Queuing-Based Modeling and Optimization of Computational Capacity for Malicious Data Detection

Hisham

Contents

List of Tables

List of Figures

1 Introduction

The rise of CAVs promises to transform modern transportation by enabling safer, more efficient, and cooperative driving. By integrating automation with advanced communication technologies, CAVs are expected to improve traffic flow, reduce accidents, and enhance overall mobility. These benefits, however, depend critically on the vehicle's ability to generate and execute control commands in real time [1] [2].

The current paradigm for automated driving largely relies on a vehicle-centric approach, where onboard sensors and computing systems independently process environmental data to guide driving decisions. While effective in many scenarios, this approach faces inherent challenges, including the computational burden of processing high-volume data inputs and the inevitable presence of natural delays in perception and control pipelines. In dynamic and safety-critical contexts, even millisecond-level delays can degrade responsiveness, increasing the risk of unsafe maneuvers [3] [4].

To address these challenges, connectivity has emerged as a central enabler. V2V and V2I communication extend situational awareness beyond what a single vehicle can perceive, creating opportunities for cooperative maneuvers and coordinated traffic management [5]. However, this same connectivity also introduces new vulnerabilities: adversaries may exploit communication protocols to generate abnormal traffic loads, causing processing slowdowns that disrupt the timely generation of control commands and compromise safety [6].

Existing research has shown that various types of cyberattacks can degrade traffic stability and vehicle responsiveness. Among these threats, one of the most concerning ones is the application-layer flooding attack, where adversaries overwhelm CAV systems with large volumes of legitimate-looking messages. Unlike traditional attacks on lower network layers, this type of flooding directly burdens onboard processors, delaying message validation and control decision-making [7]. While prior studies [8] [9] [10] [11] have measured the overall traffic-level impact of such attacks, far less is known about the mechanisms by which delays form inside the vehicle's processing pipeline.

This knowledge gap motivates the central focus of this thesis.

1.1 Background

Among these external threats, recent attention has turned to adversarial manipulation of V2V communications, where even syntactically valid messages strain system performance and cause operational delays. In contemporary CAV environments, *application-layer flooding attacks* [**?**] pose a particularly disruptive challenge. Adversaries inject large volumes of protocol-compliant but semantically misleading V2V messages to overwhelm a vehicle's onboard processing resources [7]. Unlike traditional Denial-of-Service (DoS) attacks that target lower communication layers [12], these application-layer attacks follow standard message formats but demand extensive validation. This validation process adds a heavy computational load, which increases queueing delays and prevents timely control actions [7]. These delays may compromise both traffic stability and safety in time-critical driving scenarios.

The challenge of defending against application-layer flooding comes from the structural legitimacy of the malicious messages. Traditional intrusion detection systems do not recognize these inputs because they comply with the expected formats [13]. As a result, system performance gradually deteriorates, and reliability declines. Effective countermeasures must include advanced detection tools that identify subtle inconsistencies in message content or timing, along with resilient trust management schemes that assess the credibility of incoming data [14].

Recent research has increasingly focused on how CAVs are affected by the high volume of vague or excessive V2V data, particularly under adversarial conditions. [15] showed that inconsistent or tampered messages in V2V environments can lead to safety risks and unstable traffic behavior when introducing response delay. [16] similarly highlighted how protocol-compliant but semantically uncertain messages can disrupt cooperative perception and reduce traffic flow efficiency. [17] demonstrated that abnormal V2V communication, such as the injection of misleading or redundant data, can significantly delay vehicle responses and destabilize overall network performance. [12] further analyzed how communication bottlenecks affect platooning stability, showing that message handling delay impair safety and throughput. Most recently, [7] emphasized that application-layer flooding imposes a significant computational load on onboard systems, delaying control actions. While these studies quantify the impact of adversarial V2V messaging on traffic performance, they often overlook the underlying mechanisms of delay formation within the vehicle's processing pipeline, which is critical for understanding the true nature of these disruptions.

1.2 Objectives

The background analysis has highlighted the significant challenge of delays caused by adversarial manipulation of V2V communications, specifically through application-layer flooding attacks. These attacks can strain the system's performance and delay control command generation, thus compromising the safety and efficiency of CAVs. Given the critical importance of timely processing in such systems, it is essential to understand how these delays form and how they can be mitigated.

Building on this, the primary objective of this research is to analyze how delays in control command generation arise in CAVs under adversarial conditions, with a particular focus on application-layer flooding attacks in V2V communication. While prior studies such as [8, 9, 10, 11] have quantified the impact of delays on traffic performance, they do not fully explain the mechanisms through which malicious data flooding creates computational bottlenecks within the vehicle. This thesis addresses this gap by investigating delay formation inside the CAV decision-making pipeline, rather than only at the system or traffic level.

To achieve this objective, the thesis develops a theoretical queuing-based framework that explicitly represents the sequential nature of in-vehicle data processing and control execution. The CAV data pipeline is modeled as a two-stage queue, consisting of a message filtering stage for V2V communication and a subsequent decision-making stage for control command generation. This modeling framework enables a structured analysis of how adversarial flooding amplifies processing delays and degrades vehicle responsiveness, providing a micro-level perspective that complements existing system-level approaches in the literature.

The second objective is to formulate optimization strategies for allocating finite computational resources between message filtering and control decision functions under attack, with the central aim of maximizing vehicle flow and sustaining traffic throughput even in adversarial conditions where large volumes of deceptive messages are injected into the network. This includes a fixed-budget optimization model as well as a cost-aware model that accounts for the trade-off between resilience and computational overhead. Through these formulations, the research provides actionable insights into how vehicles can maintain throughput and safety despite being targeted by application-layer flooding attacks.

Finally, the research aims to validate the proposed models through sensitivity analyses across varying system parameters such as attack intensity, traffic density and available processing power. This offers guidelines for the design of resilient CAV architectures in real-world deployment scenarios.

1.3 Scope

This thesis focuses on analyzing delays in CAVs that arise under adversarial conditions, with particular attention to flooding at the application layer of V2V communication. While natural delays from sensing, communication, and computation are acknowledged, the emphasis here is on those delays that are deliberately amplified by malicious message floods. In particular, delays arising from wireless channel effects such as propagation, interference, packet loss, or medium access contention are not explicitly modeled and are considered outside the scope of this study.

The study adopts a stylized setting in which vehicles operate on homogeneous traffic corridors with full CAV penetration. Roadside infrastructure is assumed to provide reliable connectivity, enabling the analysis to concentrate on the internal mechanisms through which message floods influence vehicle decision-making and control responsiveness.

Within this framework, the research models a two-stage decision pipeline consisting of (i) filtering incoming V2V messages and (ii) generating control commands through onboard electronic control units (ECUs). By narrowing the focus to these stages, the thesis provides a clear view of how adversarial flooding creates queuing delays that affect timely control execution.

The contribution of this research lies in its ability to connect micro-level vehicle dynamics with broader traffic performance. By investigating how delays are formed and how processing resources can be allocated to sustain responsiveness and maximizing the flow of vehicles, the research establishes a foundation for designing resilient CAV systems that maintain safety and efficiency even under attack.

The remainder of this thesis is structured as follows. Chapter 2 presents a review of related works. Chapter 3 introduces two stylized macroscopic models of a single-lane CAV corridor operating under cyberattack conditions. These models incorporate on-board, communication, and infrastructure-based sensing architectures, and represent the detection and decision-making processes as a two-stage queuing system. The chapter then derives closed-form solutions for two optimization models for resource allocation: one under a fixed compute capacity and the other with stage-specific capacity constraints. Chapter 4 presents numerical results that explore how the optimal allocations vary with vehicle density and adversarial load across different system configurations. It provides quantitative illustrations of how resources can be effectively allocated to maintain system performance. Finally, Chapter 5 summarizes the main findings and outlines potential directions for future research.

2 Literature Review

The literature on CAVs encompasses a wide range of studies that collectively form the foundation for understanding how automation, communication, and cybersecurity intersect within modern transportation systems. This section first reviews the evolution of driving automation, outlining the key technological components and levels of autonomy that define automated driving systems. It then examines the communication frameworks, such as V2V, V2I, and V2X, that enable cooperative interactions among vehicles and infrastructure. Finally, it discusses cybersecurity considerations, highlighting how increased connectivity introduces new vulnerabilities that must be addressed to ensure the safe and reliable operation of CAVs.

2.1 Automation in Driving

Automated driving has developed rapidly in recent years, enabled by advances in artificial intelligence, sensor technologies, and vehicular communication systems [18]. A CAV is an intelligent system that combines automation and connectivity to operate with minimal or no human input. It integrates an Automated Driving System (ADS) for in-vehicle autonomy and communication capabilities to enable cooperative behavior within transportation systems [19]. ADS in autonomous vehicles integrates several core functions that enable the vehicle to operate with minimal or no human intervention. Its main modules include perception, motion planning, navigation, and behavior. The perception module allows the vehicle to understand its immediate environment, detect obstacles, and assess road conditions. Motion planning translates high-level goals into executable maneuvers by controlling steering, speed, and path selection, ensuring safe and efficient travel. Navigation provides localization capabilities, combining GPS with inertial navigation systems to determine the vehicle's position and match it to road maps. Finally, the behavior module oversees decision-making, coordinating overtaking, lane-keeping, and other tactical maneuvers in real time. Together, these modules form the foundation of the ADS, enabling vehicles to process environmental data, plan safe routes, and respond dynamically to traffic conditions [20]. The next section explores the different levels of driving automation and their characteristics.

2.1.1 Levels of Automation

According to the SAE J3016 standard published by SAE International [21], driving automation refers to the functionality of systems that perform part or all of the dynamic driving task (DDT) on behalf of a human driver. These tasks include operational aspects such as steering, braking, acceleration, and monitoring the driving environment. The standard establishes a six-level taxonomy, ranging from Level 0 (no automation) to Level 5 (full automation) to classify the extent of driving support provided by such systems.

Levels 0 to 2 of driving automation involve increasing driver assistance but still require constant human supervision. Level 0 provides no automation, with the driver fully responsible. Level 1 supports either steering or speed control, and Level 2 handles both, but in all cases, the driver must monitor the environment and remain ready to take over [22]. Level 3 marks a significant shift toward conditional automation. Here, the vehicle can manage all aspects of the driving task in specific scenarios, such as highway driving, and will request human intervention when needed. The driver is not required to continuously monitor the environment but must be available to respond to system requests. At Level 4, the system is capable of handling all driving tasks within defined operational domains, such as urban ride-sharing routes or fixed shuttles, without expecting the driver to take control. If the vehicle is outside its operational limits, it will initiate a safe fallback, such as stopping [23]. Finally, Level 5 automation represents full driving autonomy. The system can perform all DDT functions under all roadway and environmental conditions without human involvement. No steering wheel or pedals are necessary in such vehicles, as human input is entirely optional [24].

This classification framework is critical for understanding the capabilities and limitations of automated driving systems and serves as a foundational reference in both industry and academic contexts [21].

2.2 Communication Technologies for Automated Driving

The emergence of CAVs comes from the integration of automation systems with robust vehicular communications. In this paradigm, Dedicated Short-Range Communications (DSRC) has been the foundational wireless technology that enables low-latency information exchange through On-Board Units (OBUs) in vehicles and Roadside Units (RSUs) embedded in infrastructure. By supporting continuous broadcast of dynamic driving information such as speed and position, DSRC makes core interaction modes like V2V and V2I communication possible and effective, ensuring that vehicles are not isolated actors but part of a cooperative mobility network [25] [26].

More recently, Cellular Vehicle-to-Everything (C-V2X) and 5G networks have been introduced as next-generation alternatives. These technologies extend the capabilities of DSRC by offering greater scalability, improved reliability, and enhanced coverage, particularly in dense urban environments. Through these advances, V2V and V2I interactions are further empowered, enabling vehicles to exchange real-time data not only for collision avoidance and intersection management but also for traffic optimization and mobility services [27] [28].

Field deployments such as the Safety Pilot Model Deployment (SPMD) in Ann Arbor, involving thousands of equipped vehicles and dozens of RSUs, have shown the robustness of these communication systems across diverse traffic and environmental conditions. The lessons from such pilots confirm that the combination of DSRC, C-V2X, and 5G technologies forms the communication backbone of CAVs, providing the foundation upon which V2V and V2I systems can operate reliably at scale[26]. In the remainder of this section, we will review the literature on different types of vehicular connectivity, followed by an examination of existing research on their benefits for enhancing automated driving.

2.2.1 V2V Communication

V2V communication plays a fundamental role in connected transportation systems by allowing nearby vehicles to exchange data directly and in real time. Unlike conventional sensors such as cameras or LiDAR, which rely on line-of-sight detection [29], V2V communication allows vehicles to share critical information, such as position, speed, and intended maneuvers, over short-range wireless networks like Dedicated Short-Range Communications (DSRC) or Cellular Vehicle-to-Everything (C-V2X) technologies [30].

Through V2V, vehicles can coordinate driving behaviors in real time, significantly improving safety and traffic efficiency. For example, by broadcasting Basic Safety Messages (BSMs) multiple times, V2V systems can alert vehicles to potential collisions, lane changes, or sudden braking events beyond the range of onboard sensors [31][32]. This predictive capability reduces reaction times, mitigating accidents caused by human delay or limited visibility [33].

Moreover, V2V forms the foundation for cooperative driving features such as platooning and Co-operative Adaptive Cruise Control (CACC), which allow groups of vehicles to travel with reduced headways while maintaining stability. These capabilities not only enhance roadway capacity but also reduce fuel consumption and emissions through smoother driving profiles[34].

2.2.2 V2I Communication

V2I communication refers to the exchange of information between connected vehicles and roadside infrastructure elements such as traffic signals, roadside units (RSUs), variable message signs, and highway sensors. This communication channel enhances traffic safety, optimizes flow, and supports advanced driving applications by delivering real-time updates about road conditions, signal timing, work zones, and congestion levels [35]. Through low-latency data sharing, V2I systems allow vehicles to anticipate and react to environmental changes well in advance, improving situational awareness and operational efficiency. For instance, Signal Phase and Timing (SPaT) messages transmitted from traffic lights enable vehicles to adjust speed for smoother intersection crossing and fuel-efficient driving patterns [36]. Furthermore, infrastructure feedback plays a crucial role in cooperative driving strategies, such as platooning and eco-driving, by coordinating maneuvers based on broader traffic insights. Studies have shown that when combined with vehicle automation and V2V systems, V2I communication significantly enhances network-wide safety and throughput by reducing stop-and-go waves and supporting real-time route optimization [37] [38].

2.2.3 V2X Communication

Vehicle-to-Everything (V2X) is a broad framework of connectivity that extends the communication capabilities of vehicles beyond what is achieved through V2V and V2I communication. While V2V and V2I form the essential building blocks of it, the "X" in V2X encompasses a wider range of entities, including on-board devices, cloud-based platforms, and even pedestrians equipped with connected devices. By integrating these diverse components, V2X transforms vehicles into active participants in a cooperative transportation network where information flows continuously to enhance safety, efficiency, and overall driving performance [5] [39].

Regulatory and safety authorities such as the National Highway Traffic Safety Administration (NHTSA) emphasize that V2X technologies can provide vehicles with a much broader awareness of their surroundings than what sensors alone can achieve. This wider situational awareness enables automated driving systems to react faster and more accurately to potential hazards, improving the reliability of advanced driver-assistance functions and automated driving features [40].

In addition to improving safety, V2X has been envisioned as a multi-service communication platform. It not only supports safety-critical use cases such as collision warnings and intersection management, but also contributes to broader objectives including smoother traffic flow [41], reduced fuel consumption [42], improved environmental sustainability [43], and enhanced compliance with traffic regulations [44]. By providing vehicles with real-time access to information from their environment, V2X plays a pivotal role in the transition toward cooperative and efficient mobility systems.

2.2.3.1 Benefits of V2V

V2V communication is fundamentally a crash-avoidance technology that markedly improves road safety. By transmitting timely warnings and vehicle state information between nearby cars, V2V allows drivers or automated systems to react to dangers much sooner than traditional onboard sensors alone. For example, V2V-equipped vehicles can see around corners or through other vehicles to detect an unseen hazard (such as a car speeding through an intersection or a sudden stop ahead) and alert drivers in advance [45]. This heightened awareness translates into fewer and less severe collisions. Studies predict that widespread implementation of V2V (as part of broader V2X systems) could prevent up to 80 percent of current road accidents by enabling more accurate and timely exchange of safety data [46]. In practical terms, such connectivity addresses human error which is the primary cause of crashes by providing early warnings for imminent threats (e.g. forward collision alerts, intersection movement assist), thereby significantly reducing crash rates and associated fatalities [46] [47]. Furthermore, the mitigation of communication delay has been shown to directly impact the effectiveness of safety systems and coordinated maneuvers, reinforcing the importance of optimized V2V protocols for reliable message delivery. These collective advantages demonstrate that V2V plays a vital role in reducing overall network delays and improving system-level traffic performance [48] [49] [50] [51].

Beyond safety, a well-documented benefit of inter-vehicle communication is improved traffic flow efficiency. V2V allows vehicles to coordinate their movements and adapt to road conditions collectively, rather than each acting in isolation. This coordination smooths out the stop-and-go waves and inefficiencies that normally arise from human reaction delays and lack of information [52]. For instance, when a V2V-equipped car several vehicles ahead brakes suddenly, it can broadcast an emergency electronic brake light alert to following cars, so they begin decelerating immediately rather than waiting to see the car in front brake [52]. Such early, networked reactions dampen traffic shockwaves and reduce unnecessary hard braking, resulting in more uniform speeds [53]. V2V communication also enables platooning, where vehicles (especially trucks or cars in a convoy) dynamically adjust their cruise control to maintain short, steady headways. By traveling in tight formation at a constant speed, platooned vehicles increase the effective road capacity, more vehicles can pass per unit time, and minimize speed fluctuations. Research surveys confirm that platooning made possible by V2V can maximally expand road throughput while shortening travel times, since vehicles can safely travel with smaller gaps and fewer interruptions [54]. One research noted that V2V-equipped cars can form platoons moving at the same speed, preventing traffic density build-ups and thus shortening overall transport time on busy corridor [54]. This translates to mitigation of congestion and delay, particularly as penetration of V2V vehicles increases in the fleet.

Empirical evidence of efficiency gains is emerging from pilot deployments. In a 2021 pilot in Georgia, two school buses were equipped with cellular V2V/V2I technology that requested green-light priority at traffic signals (communicating with intersection controllers). The connected buses experienced significantly smoother trips: a 40 percent reduction in the number of stops, a 13 percent decrease in total travel time, and an 18 percent increase in average speed compared to baseline conditions [55]. On a larger scale, simulations of connected vehicle penetration suggest that even moderate adoption of V2V-enabled adaptive cruise control could increase highway throughput and stabilize traffic stream behavior, yielding shorter commutes for many drivers [56] [57].

V2V communication also plays a significant role in reducing energy consumption and emissions through enhanced driving coordination [58]. One of the primary benefits stems from platooning, where vehicles travel closely together with minimal gaps. This formation minimizes aerodynamic drag, especially for trailing vehicles, and reduces overall fuel use. Empirical studies have demonstrated fuel savings of approximately 5–10 percent, with trailing trucks experiencing the most significant efficiency gains. Beyond platooning, V2V enables smoother traffic flow by supporting cooperative adaptive cruise control and eco-driving, where vehicles proactively adjust their speed to avoid unnecessary idling, braking, or acceleration, further conserving energy.

The benefits of V2V extend beyond connected vehicles themselves. By integrating information from both V2V and V2I sources, such as traffic signal phase and timing, vehicles can anticipate and respond to traffic conditions more efficiently. For instance, approaching vehicles can decelerate gradually when aware of red lights ahead, instead of coming to abrupt stops. This level of predictive driving not only improves the fuel efficiency of the connected vehicles but also has a harmonizing impact on nearby non-connected traffic, promoting smoother overall flow. According to recent technical reports, such communication-driven coordination significantly reduces fuel consumption and emissions at the system level, supporting broader goals for sustainable and efficient transportation networks [59] [60] [61] [62].

2.2.3.2 Benefits of V2I

V2I communication offers substantial advantages for improving transportation safety, efficiency, and sustainability. By enabling real-time data exchange between vehicles and roadway infrastructure such as traffic signals, roadside units, and dynamic signage, V2I extends the situational awareness of both human drivers and automated systems.

V2I communication represents a transformative technology that delivers multifaceted benefits across safety, efficiency, and sustainability dimensions through sophisticated real-time data exchange capabilities between vehicles and roadway infrastructure. The technology fundamentally enhances transportation systems by enabling seamless communication between vehicles and infrastructure elements such as traffic signals, RSUs, and traffic management centers, creating an interconnected ecosystem that optimizes traffic operations while prioritizing safety and environmental considerations [63]. V2I communication systems leverage advanced wireless technologies, including DSRC operating at 5.9 GHz frequencies and cellular-based solutions like LTE-V2X, to facilitate low-latency, high-reliability data transmission that supports critical safety applications and traffic optimization functions [64] [65]. The real-time data exchange capabilities enable vehicles to receive crucial information about traffic signal timing, road conditions, weather updates, and potential hazards, while simultaneously transmitting vehicle status data including position, speed, and heading to infrastructure systems for comprehensive traffic monitoring and management [66] [67].

From a safety perspective, V2I communication significantly enhances situational awareness by providing drivers and automated systems with critical information that extends beyond the line-of-sight limitations of traditional sensors. Research demonstrates that V2I systems can effectively support collision avoidance mechanisms, with studies showing up to 98 percent accuracy in classifying risky vehicles and substantial reductions in collision rates when penetration rates exceed 6 percent [68]. The technology enables infrastructure to communicate real-time hazard information, including accident locations, weather conditions, and road surface conditions, allowing vehicles to make informed decisions and take preventive actions [63]. Additionally, V2I communication supports emergency vehicle prioritization systems that can dynamically adjust traffic signal timing to provide clear corridors for emergency responders, thereby improving emergency response times and overall public safety [69]. The integration of collective perception capabilities through V2I networks allows vehicles to access information from multiple sensors deployed throughout the infrastructure, creating a comprehensive awareness system that significantly enhances safety for both vehicles and vulnerable road users [63]. Traffic signal optimization represents one of the most significant efficiency benefits of V2I communication, enabling adaptive signal control systems that respond dynamically to real-time traffic conditions rather than relying on static timing patterns. Mobile applications utilizing V2I communication can provide speed advisory systems that help drivers maintain optimal speeds to avoid stop-and-go traffic patterns at signalized intersections, thereby reducing fuel consumption and improving traffic flow [66]. Research indicates that V2I-enabled systems can achieve substantial improvements in traffic efficiency, with studies documenting travel time reductions of 10-20 percent, average speed increases of 56.12 percent, and fuel consumption reductions of 8.05 percent [70]. The technology enables sophisticated traffic management strategies, including the ability to cut red light duration or skip red phases entirely based on real-time vehicle position and timing parameters, optimizing intersection throughput while maintaining safety [71]. Furthermore, V2I communication supports coordinated traffic management across multiple intersections, enabling traffic management centers to implement system-wide optimization strategies that consider traffic patterns, congestion levels, and environmental factors [67]. The automated system integration capabilities of V2I communication create opportunities for seamless coordination between various transportation technologies and infrastructure components. V2I systems can integrate with Internet of Things (IoT) networks to provide comprehensive traffic monitoring and management capabilities, utilizing sensor networks, cameras, and other data sources to create dynamic and adaptive traffic control infrastructure [69].The technology supports the integration of electric vehicle charging management systems, enabling park-and-charge stations to optimize charging schedules and arrival rates through real-time pricing and availability information transmitted via V2I communications [72]. Advanced V2I implementations utilize machine learning algorithms and artificial intelligence to process real-time traffic data, predict traffic trends, and enable proactive management strategies that adapt to changing conditions [69]. The integration capabilities extend to support for CAV operations, where V2I communication provides essential infrastructure support for autonomous vehicle navigation and decision-making processes [73].

Sustainability benefits of V2I communication emerge through multiple mechanisms that collectively reduce the environmental impact of transportation systems. The technology enables eco-approach and departure applications that optimize vehicle speeds and timing at intersections to minimize fuel consumption and emissions, with research demonstrating CO2 emission reductions of 8.05 percent through optimized traffic flow patterns [70]. V2I communication supports the development of intelligent transportation systems that can dynamically route traffic to avoid congested areas, reducing overall fuel consumption and emissions while improving air quality in urban environments [74]. The technology facilitates the integration of environmental monitoring systems that can provide real-time information about air quality, weather conditions, and other environmental factors, enabling both infrastructure and vehicles to make environmentally conscious decisions [75]. Additionally, V2I systems support the optimization of public transportation operations through real-time data exchange between transit vehicles and traffic management centers, improving the efficiency and attractiveness of sustainable transportation modes [67].

The implementation of V2I communication systems demonstrates significant potential for transforming urban mobility through comprehensive integration of safety, efficiency, and sustainability benefits. Field testing and simulation studies consistently show that V2I technology can deliver substantial improvements across multiple performance metrics, including reduced travel times, improved fuel efficiency, enhanced safety outcomes, and decreased environmental impact [63] [66] [70].The technology's ability to support both current transportation needs and future automated vehicle deployments positions it as a critical enabler for the evolution toward smarter, more sustainable transportation systems that can adapt to changing urban mobility demands while maintaining high levels of safety and efficiency.

2.3 Cybersecurity of CAVs

This section provides an overview of the cybersecurity dimension of CAVs, examining how the increasing dependence on digital data, sensing, and connectivity exposes these systems to cyber–physical vulnerabilities. It first discusses the general importance of cybersecurity in ensuring the safe and reliable operation of CAVs, followed by a review of common attack surfaces and vulnerable components within vehicle architectures. The discussion then narrows to the specific type of cyberattack investigated in this research, application-layer flooding attacks, and analyzes their role in creating processing delays that degrade control performance, reduce vehicle flow, and compromise overall traffic efficiency.

2.3.1 Importance of Cybersecurity for CAVs

CAVs represent a fundamental transformation in transportation technology, integrating sophisticated autonomous driving capabilities with comprehensive V2X communication systems to create complex cyber-physical systems that interact seamlessly with infrastructure, other vehicles, pedestrians, and cloud-based services [76]. The cybersecurity landscape for these vehicles differs fundamentally from traditional information technology security due to their safety-critical nature, real-time operational requirements, and unique mobility characteristics, where security breaches can directly impact physical safety, potentially causing accidents, traffic disruptions, or loss of life [77]. This critical distinction elevates cybersecurity from a privacy concern to a paramount safety issue, as attacks on CAVs can have immediate and catastrophic consequences in the physical world, fundamentally altering the risk calculus for cybersecurity implementation and management [78]. The evolution of automotive systems from mechanical to electronic to connected cyber-physical systems has created unprecedented security challenges that extend far beyond traditional automotive safety considerations [79]. Modern CAVs integrate multiple complex subsystems including advanced driver assistance systems (ADAS), autonomous driving stacks, infotainment systems, telematics units, and numerous electronic control units (ECUs), each presenting potential attack vectors that can be exploited by malicious actors [80]. The integration of artificial intelligence and machine learning algorithms for perception, decision-making, and control introduces additional complexity, as these systems can be vulnerable to novel attack types such as adversarial examples that have no direct analogs in traditional cybersecurity domains [81].

The importance of cybersecurity for CAVs extends beyond individual vehicle safety to encompass broader societal implications, as demonstrated by research showing that cybersecurity concerns significantly influence consumer trust in autonomous vehicles, with perceived cyber threats negatively impacting technology acceptance and widespread deployment [82]. Consumer acceptance studies consistently demonstrate that cybersecurity concerns rank among the top barriers to autonomous vehicle adoption, with surveys indicating that potential users require strong assurances about vehicle security before they would trust these systems with their safety [83]. The psychological impact of cybersecurity incidents in the automotive domain is amplified by the personal nature of transportation and the perceived loss of control when delegating driving responsibilities to automated systems [77].

The interconnected nature of modern transportation systems means that a successful cyberattack on CAVs could cascade into larger infrastructure failures, affecting traffic management systems, emergency response capabilities, and economic activities dependent on reliable transportation networks [84] [85]. Smart city initiatives that integrate CAVs with intelligent transportation systems create dependencies where vehicle cybersecurity becomes integral to broader urban infrastructure security [86]. Traffic management systems that rely on real-time data from connected vehicles can be disrupted or manipulated through attacks on individual vehicles, potentially causing widespread traffic disruptions that extend far beyond the initially targeted vehicles [87]. Emergency response systems that depend on V2I communication for incident detection and response coordination can be compromised through attacks that interfere with or manipulate these communication channels [88].

Recent surveys indicate that cybersecurity represents one of the primary barriers to public acceptance of autonomous vehicles, creating a critical dependency between robust security implementation and successful technology adoption [80]. Market research consistently shows that consumers prioritize security and privacy concerns when considering autonomous vehicle adoption, with cybersecurity ranking alongside safety as primary decision factors [82]. The automotive industry's transition to mobility-as-a-service models and shared autonomous vehicle fleets amplifies these concerns, as security incidents affecting shared vehicles could impact multiple users and potentially damage public confidence in the entire autonomous vehicle ecosystem [89].

The high-level consequences of inadequate cybersecurity in CAVs manifest across multiple dimensions of societal impact, creating ripple effects that extend far beyond individual vehicle security incidents. Safety implications are perhaps most critical, as successful attacks could directly cause accidents, injuries, or fatalities, representing a fundamental breach of the safety assurance that autonomous vehicles are designed to provide [90]. The safety-critical nature of automotive systems means that cybersecurity failures can have immediate physical consequences, distinguishing automotive cybersecurity from other domains where security breaches typically affect only data confidentiality or system availability [91]. The potential for mass-casualty events through coordinated attacks on multiple vehicles or transportation infrastructure creates unprecedented security challenges that require new approaches to threat assessment and risk management [92].

Privacy violations represent another significant category of consequences, occurring through unauthorized access to vehicle location data, communication patterns, and personal information stored in vehicle systems, creating long-term implications for individual privacy and civil liberties [93]. Modern vehicles collect vast amounts of data about their occupants, including location histories, driving patterns, biometric data from driver monitoring systems, and personal information from connected devices and services [94]. The aggregation and analysis of this data can reveal intimate details about individuals' lives, relationships, and behaviors, creating privacy risks that extend far beyond traditional automotive concerns [95]. The potential for this data to be accessed by unauthorized parties, whether through cyberattacks or inappropriate data sharing practices, raises fundamental questions about privacy rights in the connected vehicle era [96].

Economic impacts include potential liability for manufacturers, insurance implications for vehicle owners, and broader economic disruption if attacks affect transportation infrastructure at scale [97]. The automotive industry's transition to software-defined vehicles creates new liability models where manufacturers may be held responsible for cybersecurity incidents that occur years after vehicle sale, fundamentally altering traditional product liability frameworks [46]. Insurance companies are developing new models for assessing and pricing cybersecurity risks in connected and autonomous vehicles, with cybersecurity incidents potentially affecting insurance premiums and coverage availability [98]. The economic disruption potential of large-scale cyberattacks on transportation systems could affect supply chains, emergency services, and economic activities that depend on reliable transportation infrastructure [99].

The integration of artificial intelligence and machine learning systems in CAVs introduces additional complexity to the cybersecurity landscape, as these systems can be vulnerable to novel attack types such as adversarial examples, model poisoning, and data manipulation that do not have direct analogs in traditional cybersecurity [100]. The opacity of many machine learning systems used in autonomous vehicles makes it difficult to predict how they might respond to malicious inputs, creating uncertainty about the effectiveness of defensive measures and the potential impact of successful attacks [101]. The training data dependencies of machine learning systems create new attack vectors where adversaries can compromise system behavior by manipulating training datasets or introducing biased or malicious data during the learning process [93].

Regulatory and legal frameworks for automotive cybersecurity are still evolving, creating uncertainty about compliance requirements, liability allocation, and enforcement mechanisms that complicate cybersecurity implementation efforts [97]. The global nature of the automotive industry requires harmonization of cybersecurity standards and regulations across multiple jurisdictions, each with their own legal frameworks and enforcement capabilities [90]. The long development cycles and operational lifespans of automotive systems create challenges in maintaining compliance with evolving cybersecurity regulations and standards throughout the vehicle lifecycle [85].

2.3.2 Vulnerable components and why they matter

The vulnerable components within CAVs matter because they form the foundation upon which vehicle safety and security depend, creating a complex ecosystem where the compromise of any single component can potentially cascade throughout the entire vehicle system and beyond to affect other vehicles, infrastructure, and transportation networks . The interconnected nature of modern automotive systems means that traditional security approaches focusing on perimeter defense are insufficient, requiring a comprehensive understanding of how vulnerabilities in individual components can be exploited to achieve broader attack objectives.

ECUs serve as the distributed computing nodes that control various vehicle functions, from engine management to safety systems, making their security paramount to overall vehicle integrity [102]. Modern vehicles contain between 50 to 150 ECUs, each responsible for specific functions but interconnected through various communication protocols, creating a complex distributed system where the security of individual ECUs affects the security of the entire vehicle [103]. The interconnected nature of these ECUs means that compromise of one unit can potentially cascade to others, creating systemic vulnerabilities that can affect multiple vehicle functions simultaneously[104].

The evolution from simple microcontroller-based ECUs to complex computing platforms running sophisticated software stacks has significantly expanded their attack surface and impact on vehicle security [102]. Modern ECUs can run full operating systems, support network connectivity, and execute advanced algorithms for functions such as adaptive cruise control, lane keeping assistance, and automated parking [105]. This increased computational capability also enables more sophisticated attacks, including persistent malware that can survive vehicle power cycles and propagate to other ECUs through internal networks [106].

The safety-critical nature of many ECU functions means that successful attacks can have immediate physical consequences. ECUs controlling braking, steering, acceleration, airbag deployment, and other safety systems are directly connected to vehicle operation, making their compromise a direct threat to occupants and other road users. The real-time requirements of safety-critical ECUs also limit the computational overhead available for security measures, constraining the types of defenses that can be implemented [107].

Supply chain complexity adds further security challenges, as ECUs integrate hardware and software from multiple suppliers with varying security practices. Long development cycles can result in the use of platforms that are outdated or contain known vulnerabilities by the time a vehicle reaches end-of-life. Moreover, difficulties in updating ECU firmware mean that security weaknesses may persist for the lifetime of the vehicle, creating long-term risks [108].

Advanced attacks may exploit hardware vulnerabilities, such as side-channel attacks to extract cryptographic keys, or use fault injection to bypass security checks and execute unauthorized code. ECU-specific malware that persists in non-volatile memory and survives firmware updates represents an emerging threat capable of significantly impacting vehicle security [109].

Sensor systems including cameras, LiDAR, radar, and GPS receivers are critical because they provide the environmental awareness necessary for autonomous operation, and their compromise can lead to fundamental misunderstanding of the vehicle's surroundings, potentially causing the vehicle to make dangerous decisions based on false or manipulated sensor data [21]. These sensors form the eyes and ears of autonomous vehicles, translating physical environmental conditions into digital data that drives decision-making algorithms [109]. The criticality of sensor integrity cannot be overstated, as even minor compromises in sensor data can lead to catastrophic misinterpretations of the driving environment [110].

Camera systems in autonomous vehicles are vulnerable to various attacks, including adversarial examples that cause misclassification, lighting-based attacks that confuse sensors, and physical attacks that damage or obstruct lenses [110]. As autonomous driving increasingly relies on computer vision, ensuring camera security is critical [111]. The use of multiple cameras for stereo and surround-view monitoring adds complexity to securing these systems while maintaining real-time performance [112]. Integration of AI and machine learning for perception introduces further risks, such as adversarial machine learning, where crafted inputs mislead AI, and vulnerabilities in training data that can bias or compromise system behavior [113]. The black-box nature of many vision AI systems makes predicting responses to attacks difficult, complicating defense strategies [114].

LiDAR systems, while harder to compromise than cameras, remain susceptible to spoofing attacks that introduce false distance readings, potentially fabricating or concealing obstacles [115]. Their reliance on precise, coherent laser light makes them vulnerable to interference from both malicious laser sources and nearby LiDAR-equipped vehicles [116]. High cost and system complexity often limit redundancy and built-in security measures. More advanced LiDAR spoofing threats go beyond single-scan disturbances; for instance, Physical Removal Attacks can persistently erase real obstacle point clouds, evading detection across consecutive LiDAR cycles and even fooling multi-sensor fusion systems [117]. Furthermore, coordinated attacks exploiting LiDAR in combination with other sensors pose additional challenges, as adversaries may need to spoof multiple sensor types simultaneously for effectiveness [118].

Radar systems used for functions such as adaptive cruise control, blind spot monitoring, and collision avoidance are vulnerable to jamming and spoofing attacks that can interfere with object detection and distance measurement [119]. The radio frequency nature of radar systems makes them susceptible to interference from other radio sources, both intentional and unintentional [120]. The growing density of radar-equipped vehicles on modern roads amplifies the risk of mutual interference, which can not only degrade sensing reliability but also conceal intentional jamming or spoofing attacks [121].

GPS receivers in autonomous vehicles are highly vulnerable to spoofing due to their weak satellite signals, which attackers can overpower with modest equipment. Spoofing can mislead vehicles about their true position, causing navigation errors or enabling location-based attacks. More advanced techniques can drift perceived positions gradually, making detection difficult [122]. While integration with inertial navigation and other modalities increases resilience, it also creates new opportunities for coordinated multi-sensor attacks [123]. Given GPS's central role in providing real-time global positioning that supports lane-level vehicle localization and map matching for autonomous navigation , often in combination with high-definition maps and additional sensors, its vulnerabilities pose significant risks to the safety and reliability of autonomous vehicle operations[124] [125], [126] [127].

Communication interfaces such as V2X radios, cellular modems, Wi-Fi, and Bluetooth modules serve as the primary attack surfaces for remote exploitation, as they can be accessed without physical proximity to the vehicle. These interfaces enable the connectivity that defines modern connected vehicles but simultaneously expose pathways for attackers to infiltrate vehicle systems. Their wireless nature makes them inherently vulnerable to eavesdropping, jamming, and injection attacks that can be carried out from a distance [102] [104].

V2X systems are particularly critical because of their role in cooperative driving and traffic management. However, their broadcast nature makes them susceptible to message injection and flooding attacks, where adversaries overwhelm the communication channel with excessive or false messages. Such flooding can degrade system performance or prevent legitimate safety messages from being processed in time, creating denial-of-service conditions with direct safety implications . Additionally, the real-time nature of V2X limits the computational overhead available for strong cryptographic protections, making defenses against these attacks even more challenging [107] [128] [129].

Beyond V2X, other wireless modules such as cellular modems, Wi-Fi, and Bluetooth interfaces introduce further risks. Cellular modems, essential for over-the-air updates and cloud services, can be exploited through vulnerabilities in cellular infrastructure or rogue base stations. Similarly, Wi-Fi and Bluetooth, often used for consumer convenience features, may lack hardened security protocols suitable for safety-critical automotive contexts. Weak implementations, combined with the proliferation of connected consumer devices, create opportunities for attackers to exploit these channels as entry points into vehicle networks . The growing reliance on 5G adds complexity by expanding the attack surface through features such as network slicing and edge computing [130] [131] [107].

Understanding why these vulnerable components matter provides the foundation for developing effective security strategies that can protect both individual vehicles and the broader transportation ecosystem [132]. The complexity and interconnected nature of these vulnerabilities require coordinated efforts from vehicle manufacturers, technology suppliers, infrastructure operators, and regulatory bodies to ensure that the promise of safe, efficient autonomous transportation can be realized without compromising security or public safety [133]. The ongoing evolution of both attack techniques and defensive capabilities suggests that understanding and protecting these vulnerable components will remain a critical area of focus as CAV technologies continue to mature and achieve widespread deployment.

2.3.3 Attack Types Targeting CAVs

Cyberattacks on CAVs can be broadly classified into two categories: intra-vehicle network attacks and inter-vehicle network attacks. This classification reflects whether the attack exploits vulnerabilities inside the vehicle's internal communication architecture or in the external wireless communication channels that connect it to other vehicles and infrastructure [134].

Intra-vehicle network attacks target the internal wired and wireless subsystems that allow the different electronic control units (ECUs) and onboard systems to communicate. These include the Controller Area Network (CAN), Local Interconnect Network (LIN), FlexRay, Media Oriented Systems Transport (MOST), and automotive Ethernet [135]. Because these systems govern critical functions such as braking, acceleration, and steering, any malicious intrusion into them can have immediate safety implications [136]. Such attacks are often executed through direct physical access, either via onboard diagnostic (OBD-II) ports or through compromised components already installed in the vehicle [137]. Once inside, attackers can inject unauthorized messages onto the CAN bus to override driver commands, manipulate sensor readings to mislead safety systems, or even disable essential functionalities [138]. In some cases, attackers exploit weaknesses in infotainment systems or Bluetooth connections to gain a foothold in the in-vehicle network before moving laterally to safety-critical ECUs [139]. While these attacks can be highly damaging, their reliance on physical access or a pre-compromised internal node limits their scalability, making them more targeted in nature rather than widespread threats across a fleet.

Inter-vehicle network attacks, in contrast, exploit the wireless communication links used for V2X interactions, particularly V2V and V2I communications. These systems are typically implemented using DSRC or Cellular Vehicle-to-Everything (C-V2X) technologies and are fundamental to modern intelligent transportation systems [140]. Because V2X communications rely on broadcast messages exchanged in real time between multiple parties, an attacker can remotely influence not just a single vehicle but entire groups of vehicles simultaneously, often without being physically close to the target [141]. A variety of attack strategies have been identified in this category. In message spoofing, an attacker sends false position, speed, or hazard data to create the impression of traffic congestion, accidents, or other dangerous conditions that do not exist, prompting unnecessary or unsafe maneuvers [142]. Replay attacks involve capturing valid safety messages and retransmitting them at a later time, misleading vehicles into responding to outdated information [143]. Sybil attacks occur when a malicious actor forges multiple false identities in the network, distorting cooperative algorithms such as those used for congestion management or platoon formation [144]. Denial-of-Service (DoS) and jamming attacks seek to overwhelm the communication channel with noise or excessive data, causing delays or preventing the delivery of critical safety messages [9] [145]. Man-in-the-Middle (MitM) attacks allow adversaries to intercept and modify legitimate communications between vehicles or between a vehicle and infrastructure, potentially altering safety-critical information in transit [146]. Another form of attack, sensor spoofing, manipulates external perception systems such as GNSS, LiDAR, or cameras, feeding them fabricated inputs to deceive automated driving functions [147] [116].

2.3.4 Application-layer Flooding Attack

Within the spectrum of inter-vehicle network threats, one particularly disruptive class is the application-layer flooding attack. Unlike conventional DoS attacks that target the lower layers of the communication stack, flooding attacks at the application layer operate by sending large volumes of messages that are syntactically valid and conform to established V2V communication protocols[7]. In this type of attack, an adversary transmits an abnormally high number of Basic Safety Messages (BSMs), Cooperative Awareness Messages (CAMs), or other application-specific packets at a rate significantly exceeding the standardized limit, often more than the usual 10 Hz interval used in DSRC systems [9]. Because the messages follow legitimate formats and protocol rules, they bypass many intrusion detection systems, which often rely on syntax or format validation. The receiving vehicles treat these packets as genuine, dedicating processing resources to verify and interpret them. This imposes a substantial computational load on onboard systems, causing the message processing queue to grow and delaying the execution of time-critical driving decisions.

The impact of application-layer flooding is not limited to onboard processing [7]. In DSRC networks, an excessive number of high-priority application messages can saturate the 10 MHz control channel, increasing the rate of packet collisions and reducing the probability that legitimate safety messages will be delivered within strict latency requirements [59]. In C-V2X Mode 4 networks, flooding attacks can disrupt the semi-persistent scheduling (SPS) mechanism, which is responsible for allocating time–frequency resources for message transmission. By monopolizing these resources with unnecessary messages, an attacker can block legitimate vehicles from reserving slots, further degrading communication reliability [148].

Recent research has demonstrated the severity of these effects. [149] showed that adversarial V2V traffic can cause significant delays in cooperative driving responses, increasing the risk of collisions. [16] found that even when messages are syntactically correct, high volumes of uncertain or misleading information can impair cooperative perception and reduce traffic flow efficiency. [17] reported that abnormal V2V communication patterns, such as excessive message injection, can destabilize overall network performance and delay emergency responses. [12] analyzed the effect of communication bottlenecks on vehicle platooning, demonstrating that delays in message handling directly undermine both safety and throughput. Most recently, [7] emphasized that application-layer flooding can create substantial internal processing delays even when the physical communication channel remains unaffected, underscoring its unique threat profile compared to traditional DoS methods.

Given their ability to bypass conventional defenses, disrupt critical safety applications, and degrade both communication and decision-making performance, application-layer flooding attacks represent a serious operational threat to CAV ecosystems. Understanding how these attacks impact the internal processing pipeline of connected vehicles and how to optimally allocate limited onboard computational resources to detection and control under such conditions is therefore essential for ensuring the resilience and reliability of future intelligent transportation systems.

2.3.4.1 Delay

In CAVs, the generation of control commands relies on data collected from onboard sensors alongside information exchanged via V2V and V2I communication. These inputs must be fused and interpreted by ECUs before being transformed into actionable commands [150]. Because of the sequential nature of this pipeline, delays can arise at multiple stages, including sensor acquisition, wireless transmission, and ECU processing. Even small disruptions in timing can reduce responsiveness and undermine safety-critical maneuvers [151].

Natural delays are particularly evident in the handling of high-resolution and high-bandwidth sensor data. Cameras and LiDAR, for example, generate large volumes of information that require intensive pre-processing, while localization and perception systems often depend on computationally demanding sensor [152]. Each of these steps introduces latency on the order of milliseconds, which accumulate before a control command is issued. Though generally manageable, these latencies can still affect performance in time-sensitive scenarios, especially when combined with the variability of wireless channels or transient network congestion [153] [154].

Also, further latency arises from communication with external entities. V2V and V2I communications are subject to wireless transmission constraints, including medium access delays, interference, and packet retransmissions [151]. Even without malicious interference, network congestion and channel contention can slow down the delivery of safety-critical messages. Encryption and authentication processes, while necessary for security, also contribute additional milliseconds of processing delay . In cooperative maneuvers such as platooning or intersection negotiation, these communication-induced latencies can significantly affect coordination among vehicles [155].

The accumulation of delays in sensing and communication translates directly into lag within the control pipeline. Autonomous vehicles rely on rapid feedback loops to track planned trajectories, adjust speed, and avoid obstacles. When delays occur, control algorithms act on outdated data, which can reduce precision or destabilize vehicle responses. Even small latencies in adaptive cruise control can increase braking distance, while trajectory tracking under delay may lead to path deviation. Thus, natural delays, though often short, can have critical effects on real-time safety and performance [156] [157] [158] [159].

At the same time, the very sensitivity of CAVs to timing disruptions creates a broader vulnerability: delays need not arise solely from natural causes. Adversaries can deliberately exploit these weaknesses, introducing harmful latencies through targeted cyberattacks that degrade responsiveness and compromise safety [160]. These attack-induced delays are particularly concerning in V2V contexts, where the timely exchange of safety-critical information is essential. Numerous studies have shown that cyberattacks on V2V links can degrade traffic flow and vehicle responsiveness, often quantified through delay-related metrics [161] [50].

Although numerous cyberattacks are capable of inducing harmful delays, application-layer flooding attacks are especially disruptive. Accordingly, this work concentrates on analyzing their impact, with particular emphasis on how they contribute to delays in control command generation. This attack, also known as Layer 7 Distributed Denial of Service (DDoS) attacks, pose significant threats to the performance and safety of CAVs. These attacks target the application layer of the OSI model, aiming to overwhelm vehicle systems by sending a high volume of seemingly legitimate messages. Unlike traditional flooding attacks that focus on network resources, application-layer attacks exploit the application layer's protocols and services, making them more challenging to detect and mitigate[162]. As autonomous vehicle systems rely heavily on complex communication protocols, vulnerabilities at the application layer can have cascading impacts on vehicle functionality and safety, making detection and mitigation more difficult [163].

The delay introduced by these attacks occurs as the malicious messages flood the system, occupying computational resources that are typically allocated for critical safety functions [9]. As a result, even small delays in processing these messages can lead to significant consequences in real-time operations. These delays can directly impact the vehicle's ability to detect and respond to obstacles, traffic signals, and other dynamic factors that influence safe driving [164]. The disruption of communication channels between vehicles and infrastructure further exacerbates the problem, impairing the vehicle's situational awareness and response time [78].

As the scale of autonomous vehicle deployment increases, these attacks will become more frequent and sophisticated. Advanced techniques like oversized Basic Safety Messages (BSMs) and UDP flooding attacks can overwhelm the system and delay the delivery of crucial safety signals. The study by [9] underscores the severity of these delays, which can prevent vehicles from performing essential safety functions like automatic emergency braking or collision avoidance. This could lead to an increased risk of accidents and harm to vehicle occupants and pedestrians.

Mitigating the effects of application-layer flooding attacks on CAVs requires an advanced approach to both detection and prevention. As traditional intrusion detection systems often fail to flag these types of attacks due to their legitimate message format [165], alternative anomaly detection mechanisms that analyze transmission patterns [166], timing inconsistencies [167], or frequency of data inflow are necessary.

In conclusion, application-layer flooding attacks represent a significant cybersecurity threat to the performance and safety of CAVs. The resulting delays in processing and control command generation can impair the vehicle's ability to respond to dynamic driving conditions, thereby compromising safety [9]. Continued research and development of advanced detection and mitigation strategies are essential to enhance the resilience of CAV systems against these sophisticated attacks.

In the next chapter, we propose two modeling frameworks designed to minimize these delay effects while simultaneously maximizing vehicle flow and speed, providing a balanced approach to improving both traffic performance and operational safety.

3 Queuing-based Modeling

This study considers a single-lane corridor designated exclusively for CAVs. Each vehicle acquires information through onboard sensors, V2V communication, and V2I systems embedded within the corridor. These infrastructure-based elements operate as stationary data sources that enhance environmental awareness. The corridor remains free of unexpected obstructions, and access is restricted to CAVs to ensure controlled conditions. Vehicle movement follows the structure imposed by the available data and the allocation of processing capacity between detection and decision-making functionalities. To capture the dynamics of this controlled environment, the model relates vehicle velocity to density, communication limitations, and processing capacity, while incorporating safety constraints and flow efficiency considerations. Building on this foundation, the remainder of the chapter develops the model step by step using principles from queueing theory, culminating in two optimization frameworks and corresponding closed-form expressions that characterize optimal processing allocations under varying conditions.

3.1 Queuing System

The system under consideration consists of two sequential queueing stages: detection and decision-making. Each stage is characterized by specific data processing responsibilities within the overall cyber-physical infrastructure. First, the detection station receives the raw V2V stream, inspects every packet, and determine whether it is malicious or benign, and then drops any malicious packets while passing the benign ones to the next stage for further processing.

Let $\lambda_v(S)$ and μ_v denote the arrival rate and service rate of V2V data at the detection station, respectively. We define:

$$\lambda_v(S) = \begin{cases} \lambda_v, & \text{if } S < r \\ 0, & \text{if } S \geq r \end{cases} \tag{1}$$

The parameter S denotes the spacing between a subject vehicle and its neighboring connected vehicle. This formulation ensures that V2V data arrivals occur only when the inter-vehicle spacing S is within the V2V communication range r. In our model, r serves a dual role: it denotes both the V2V communication range and the onboard sensor range, reflecting the furthest distance over which a vehicle can detect or receive information about others. The arrival of V2V packets, while dependent on inter-vehicle spacing S, also varies in computational impact depending on the nature of the packets. Some packets are benign and require standard processing, whereas others are malicious and impose a heavier load on the detection station. To capture this effect, we define the effective arrival rate at the detection stage as

$$\lambda_v^{\text{det}} = (1-\alpha)\lambda_v + C_m \cdot \alpha \cdot \lambda_v, \tag{2}$$

where $C_m \geq 1$ represents the relative processing cost of a malicious packet compared to a benign one. The first term, $(1-\alpha)\lambda_v$, corresponds to the portion of benign packets that require standard processing, while the second term, $C_m \cdot \alpha \cdot \lambda_v$, captures the extra resources consumed by malicious packets. This formulation reflects that malicious packets, though proportionally fewer, impose a disproportionately higher load on the detection stage, thereby increasing queueing delays and impacting the timeliness of control command generation.

Next, let λ_{total} and μ_{t} represent the arrival rate and service rate at the decision-making station, where λ_{total} includes the arrival of both V2I and onboard sensor data showing by λ_{t} and a portion of refined V2V data.

The average waiting time at each queue can be derived using the M/M/1/∞ queuing model, where the expected waiting time is given as:

$$W_v = \frac{1}{\mu_v - \lambda_v^{det}} = \frac{1}{\mu_v - [(1-\alpha)\lambda_v + C_m \cdot \alpha \cdot \lambda_v]}, \tag{3}$$

$$W_t = \frac{1}{\mu_t - \lambda_{\text{total}}} = \frac{1}{\mu_t - (\beta(S)(1-\alpha)\lambda_v(S) + \lambda_t)}. \tag{4}$$

Here, W_v and W_t denote the average waiting times at the detection and decision-making queues, respectively. $\beta(S)$ reflects the importance of the refined V2V data in the decision-making process. To capture how this relevance decays as vehicles spread out, we define $\beta(S)$ as a piecewise-linear function over the spacing interval $[\ell, r]$, where ℓ is the minimum safety distance:

$$\beta(S) = \begin{cases} 1 - \frac{S-\ell}{r-\ell}, & \text{if } \ell \leq S < r, \\ 0, & \text{if } S \geq r. \end{cases} \tag{5}$$

This formulation assumes that V2V data is fully effective when spacing is minimal (i.e., $S = \ell$), and gradually loses utility as spacing approaches the maximum communication threshold r. Beyond this point, vehicles are assumed to fall outside the effective communication range, and $\beta(S)$ is set to zero. The linear decay structure ensures both interpretability and analytical tractability, while capturing the spatially dependent nature of cooperative data exchange. Beyond spatial relevance, the trustworthiness of received V2V data is also critical to the system's performance. The parameter $\alpha \in [0, 1]$ represents the proportion of malicious or corrupted V2V packets in the incoming data stream. Together with $\beta(S)$, it modulates the effective V2V load entering the decision-making process, accounting for both data quality and spatial relevance.

Furthermore, we consider T representing a constant time delay in capturing the vehicle's response time for executing the control command after its generation. Accordingly, the total waiting time in the system, denoted by τ, consists of the waiting times at both stations, along with the fixed execution time T. This can be expressed as:

$$\tau = \begin{cases} \frac{1}{\mu_v - [(1-\alpha)\lambda_v + C_m \cdot \alpha \cdot \lambda_v]} + \frac{1}{\mu_t - [(1 - \frac{S-\ell}{r-\ell})(1-\alpha)\lambda_v + \lambda_t]} + T, & S < r, \\ \frac{1}{\mu_t - \lambda_t} + T, & S \geq r, \end{cases} \tag{6}$$

(7)

The piecewise structure of the function reflects our modeling assumption regarding the availability of V2V data. Specifically, when the spacing S between vehicles is less than the communication threshold r, vehicles are able to receive V2V packets, and the total delay includes both the detection and decision-making stages along with the fixed execution time T. However, when $S \geq r$, vehicles are assumed to be outside the effective V2V range and thus do not receive V2V messages. In this case, the detection stage is effectively bypassed and the delay reduces to the queueing delay at the decision-making station plus the fixed execution time T. This formulation ensures that the model adapts to connectivity conditions and avoids attributing unnecessary delay to the detection stage when no inter-vehicle information is available.

We now turn to the overall system structure that governs processing delays. The flowchart in Figure 1 provides a detailed view of our two-stage processing pipeline. Raw V2V packets arrive at the detection station, where a fraction α of messages may be malicious and are filtered out, yielding delay W_v. The remaining packets, weighted by the spacing-dependent function $\beta(S)$, merge with V2I and onboard sensor data and enter the decision-making station, where delay W_t is incurred before control commands are produced. Finally, an additional fixed processing overhead T, represents the actuation and execution time. This end-to-end representation quantifies how adversarial load, spatial relevance, and execution overhead combine to determine total processing latency τ. With this framework in place, we now derive the resulting speed–density and flow–density relationships in the next section.

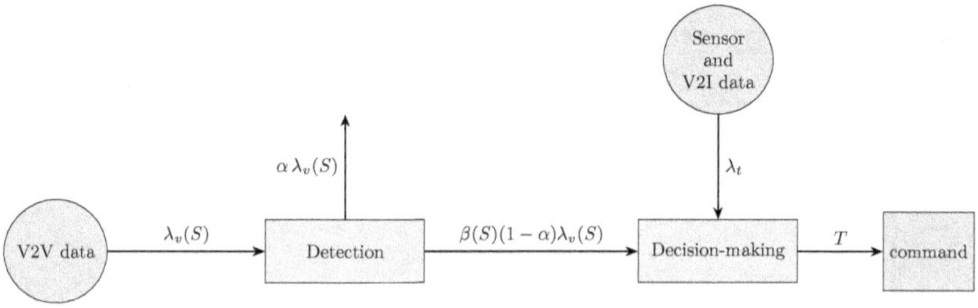

Figure 1: Flowchart of data filtering and decision-making processes

3.2 Queuing-based Speed and Flow Formulation

In a CAV system, the effective velocity of a vehicle is influenced not only by physical traffic conditions but also by the delays induced by data processing across the system. These processing delays increase the total time required for data to traverse the system and consequently reduce the achievable vehicle velocity.

Following the queueing-based modeling framework, the velocity of a CAV is inversely proportional to the total processing delay τ, scaled by the effective reaction distance available ahead. This reaction space is defined as $\min(S,r)-\ell$, where S is the average vehicle spacing, ℓ is a fixed safety buffer, and r represents both V2V communication range and on-board sensor range.

We consider a restricted-access corridor exclusively used by CAVs. This setting ensures homogeneous traffic behavior, full vehicle cooperation, and uninterrupted communication availability. Importantly, we assume no stationary obstacles or unexpected intrusions can appear along the corridor. This assumption is justified by infrastructure control (e.g., physical barriers, monitored entry) and enables a predictive model where vehicles only need to react to other moving agents. Under these conditions, the safe velocity of a vehicle depends on its awareness of leading vehicles, which is governed by communication capabilities and inter-vehicle spacing. The resulting velocity expression is:

$$V = \frac{\min(S,r)-\ell}{\tau}. \tag{8}$$

This structure enables the model to account for both physical (spacing, safety) and cyber (latency, communication) constraints in determining safe operating speeds. To reformulate this relationship regarding vehicle density, we substitute $k=\frac{1}{S}$, resulting in an expression for velocity as a function of k.

$$V = \begin{cases} \dfrac{r-\ell}{\dfrac{1}{\mu_t - \lambda_t} + T}, & k \le \frac{1}{r}, \\[2ex] \dfrac{1-k\ell}{k\left[\dfrac{1}{\mu_v - [(1-\alpha)\lambda_v + C_m \cdot \alpha \cdot \lambda_v]} + \dfrac{1}{\mu_t - \left[\frac{kr-1}{k(r-\ell)}(1-\alpha)\lambda_v + \lambda_t\right]} + T\right]}, & k > \frac{1}{r}. \end{cases} \tag{9}$$

This formulation distinguishes between two traffic conditions. When $k \le \frac{1}{r}$, vehicles maintain spacing greater than the V2V communication range, which limits perception but allows movement at the maximum safe speed. In $k > \frac{1}{r}$, the reduced spacing places greater demand on local awareness, and the speed decreases as density rises. The formula accommodates physical and cyber constraints and reflects system behavior under varying traffic environments. Figure 2(a) illustrates the resulting speed–density diagram. For clarity, simplified notation is adopted for the delay terms. The delay associated with the decision-making process is denoted by τ_t, while the total processing delay applicable when $K > \frac{1}{r}$ is denoted by τ_{total}.

Building on the velocity expression, the traffic flow Q is defined as the product of vehicle density and speed, following the fundamental relationship:

$$Q = k \cdot V.$$

Substituting the queueing-based expression for V, the flow becomes a nonlinear, influenced by the vehicle spacing, the extent of the reaction range r, cyber attack parameters such as α, and the available processing capacities μ_v and μ_t. As density increases, delays induced by queuing and cyber-physical constraints reduce speed, which in turn limits flow. This results in a unimodal flow–density relationship that captures both free-flow and congestion regimes endogenously.

$$Q = \begin{cases} K \cdot \dfrac{r-\ell}{\dfrac{1}{\mu_t - \lambda_t} + T}, & k \le \frac{1}{r}, \\ \dfrac{1-k\ell}{\dfrac{1}{\mu_v - [(1-\alpha)\lambda_v + C_m \cdot \alpha \cdot \lambda_v]} + \dfrac{1}{\mu_t - \left[\frac{kr-1}{k(r-\ell)}(1-\alpha)\lambda_v + \lambda_t\right]} + T}, & k > \frac{1}{r}. \end{cases} \tag{10}$$

Based on the derived piecewise expression for flow Q, we define the capacity of the corridor, denoted by F, as the maximum achievable flow:

$$F = \max_K Q. \tag{11}$$

The value of K at which this maximum occurs is known as the critical density:

$$K^{cr} = \arg\max_K Q. \tag{12}$$

In our model, the critical density occurs precisely at $k^{cr} = \frac{1}{r}$, where queueing delays begin to dominate. Figure 2(b) illustrates the flow–density diagram resulting from our model. The left branch of the curve corresponds to the regime where traffic flows freely without significant delays, where increased density leads to higher flow due to improved connectivity and efficient data exchange. In this region, vehicles can maintain relatively high speeds, and as density increases, flow also increases due to the benefits of enhanced communication and data exchange. As the density approaches the critical density k^{cr}, a drop in the flow and velocity is observed. This drop arises from the transition between the free-flow regime and the onset of congestion. The jump is caused by the shift in traffic dynamics when the system begins to experience queueing delays and cyber-induced traffic disruptions. Beyond this point, further increases in density lead to a decrease in flow. This decline occurs as queueing delays grow due to limited processing resources and increased exposure to adversarial data. The system's flow is constrained by these delays, which cause vehicles to slow down and reduce the overall throughput, reflecting the onset of congestion driven by both physical and cyber-physical dynamics.

While Figure 2 resemble classical fundamental diagrams, their shapes in our model are derived from queuing-based delay functions that depend on vehicle density and processing load. Specifically, speed and flow are defined via nonlinear expressions (Equations 9 and 10), and are not assumed *a priori* to follow linear or triangular forms. The observed shapes emerge naturally from the underlying queuing delays and are analytically justified by examining the first and second derivatives $\frac{\partial V}{\partial k}, \frac{\partial Q}{\partial k}, \frac{\partial^2 V}{\partial k^2}, \frac{\partial^2 Q}{\partial k^2}$ in appendices A and B , which confirm the expected monotonic trends under realistic parameter settings.

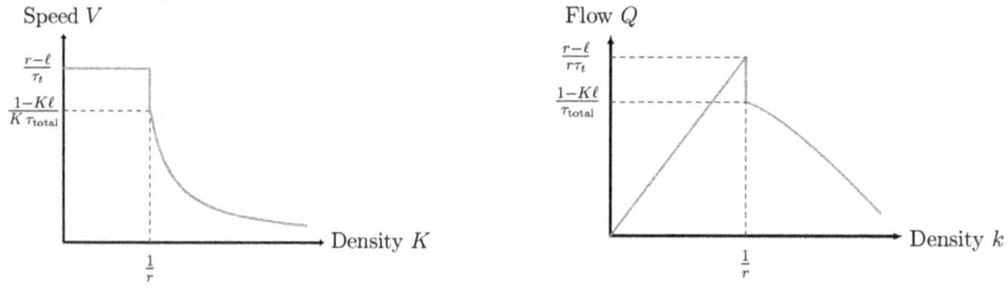

Figure 2: (a) Speed–density and (b) flow–density diagrams

3.3 Optimization Model

To optimize the allocation of onboard processing power between detection and decision-making tasks, we develop two optimization models grounded in queueing theory. These models capture the sequential nature of the vehicle's data processing pipeline, where incoming V2V messages are first filtered for malicious content before being fused with sensor and infrastructure inputs to generate control decisions. By modeling each stage as a service queue and incorporating the effects of adversarial traffic, we derive tractable formulations that quantify the impact of processing allocations on overall system performance. The first model assumes a fixed computational budget, while the second introduces cost-aware flexibility in resource usage. Both frameworks aim to maximize traffic throughput while ensuring stability and responsiveness under attack.

3.3.1 Fixed Computational Capacity (FCC) Model

In this study, the onboard processing of a CAV is represented by two sequential stations: a detection station that filters incoming V2V messages, followed by a decision making station that fuses the filtered data with V2I and sensor inputs to generate control commands. Under application-layer flooding, allocating too little capacity to the detection station allows malicious packets to overwhelm the decision stage, whereas over-allocating to security unnecessarily delays command generation. To resolve this trade-off, we develop a theoretical optimization framework that, given a fixed total service rate budget C, calculates the optimal split (μ_v, μ_t) between detection and decision-making that maximizes vehicle flow in our model corridor despite attack-induced delays. The resulting optimization model is presented below.

$$\max_{\mu_v,\mu_t} \quad \frac{1}{S}\frac{\min(S,r)-\ell}{\tau} \tag{13}$$

$$\text{s.t.} \quad \tau = \begin{cases} \frac{1}{\mu_v-\lambda_v^{det}} + \frac{1}{\mu_t-[(1-\frac{S-\ell}{r-\ell})(1-\alpha)\lambda_v(S)+\lambda_t]} + T, & S<r, \\ \frac{1}{\mu_t-\lambda_t} + T, & S \geq r, \end{cases} \tag{14}$$

$$\lambda_v^{\text{det}} = \lambda_v(1-\alpha) + \lambda_v C_m \alpha, \tag{15}$$

$$\mu_v > \lambda_v^{det}, \tag{16}$$

$$\mu_t > \beta(S)(1-\alpha)\lambda_v(S) + \lambda_t, \tag{17}$$

$$\mu_v + \mu_t = C, \tag{18}$$

$$0 \leq \alpha \leq 1, \tag{19}$$

$$\beta(S) = \begin{cases} 1-\frac{S-\ell}{r-\ell}, & S<r, \\ 0, & S \geq r, \end{cases} \tag{20}$$

$$\lambda_v(S) = \begin{cases} \lambda_v, & S<r, \\ 0, & S \geq r, \end{cases} \tag{21}$$

$$\mu_v, \mu_t \geq 0. \tag{22}$$

Constraint (16) ensures that the detection station has sufficient capacity to process incoming V2V messages. Specifically, to resist an application-layer flooding attack, the detection stage must provide enough throughput to handle the heavy attack-induced V2V load and keep the first-stage queue stable; otherwise backlog grows without bound and the downstream decision stage becomes overwhelmed. Constraint (17) guarantees that the decision-making station can handle the combined data stream it receives. The required throughput μ_t must be large enough to accommodate refined V2V data, infrastructure-based information (V2I), and onboard sensor inputs. Without this condition, the second stage could become a bottleneck, resulting in unbounded delays. Constraint (18) is motivated by standard principles in queueing theory. We assume a policy that never idles a server while a job waits and assign no explicit cost to capacity. Under these conditions, performance measures such as delay, queue length, loss, and abandonment are monotone in service capacity, meaning that any feasible increase in capacity at a congested stage cannot worsen performance. Consequently, an optimal solution will always exhaust the available budget, and the two capacities must sum exactly to the fixed resource limit [168] [169] [170]. This constraint enforces full utilization of the vehicle's onboard processing resources and encodes the trade-off: any increase in detection throughput μ_v necessarily comes at the expense of decision-making throughput μ_t, and vice versa. Finally, the feasible ranges of the malicious data proportion α is restricted between 0 and 1, consistent with its interpretation as normalized proportion. Together, these constraints define the feasible region of the problem. They ensure stability at each stage, enforce efficient use of the vehicle's onboard processing capacity, and capture the trade-offs inherent in capacity allocation. The resulting optimization model is a nonlinear program with linear and piecewise-defined constraints, and its objective function is concave, as shown in Appendix C.

Lemma 1: Following the earlier formulation of queueing model, we now derive the optimal service rates μ_v^* and μ_t^* for the detection station v and decision-making station t, respectively. The optimal service rates by setting $\frac{\partial Q}{\partial \mu_v} = 0$ and $\frac{\partial Q}{\partial \mu_t} = 0$ give:

$$\mu_v^* = \begin{cases} \frac{C+\lambda_v[1+\alpha(C_m-1)]-\left(1-\frac{S-\ell}{r-\ell}\right)(1-\alpha)\lambda_v-\lambda_t}{2}, & \text{if } S < r \\ 0, & \text{if } S \geq r \end{cases} \quad (23)$$

$$\mu_t^* = \begin{cases} \frac{C-\lambda_v[1+\alpha(C_m-1)]+\left(1-\frac{S-\ell}{r-\ell}\right)(1-\alpha)\lambda_v+\lambda_t}{2}, & \text{if } S < r \\ C, & \text{if } S \geq r \end{cases} \quad (24)$$

Proof of lemma 1 is provided in Appendix D.

3.3.2 Cost-Aware Capacity Allocation (CAC) Model

We now introduce an alternative optimization framework that relaxes the fixed-budget constraint of the previous model. We treat the detection and decision service rates as independently adjustable, each bounded above by platform-imposed limits rather than enforcing a hard equality between total onboard processing capacity and its allocation across modules. The objective is to maximize traffic flow while balancing two forces, delay-induced performance degradation along the pipeline and the computational expense of higher processing rates. The latter is represented with linear coefficients C_1 and C_2, which assign per-unit costs to detection and decision capacity, respectively, capturing energy draw, thermal headroom, and contention with other onboard tasks [170]. This cost-aware relaxation reflects real-world trade-offs between performance and resource expenditure. The revised mathematical model is presented below.

$$\max_{\mu_v,\mu_t} \quad \frac{1}{S} \cdot \frac{\min(S,r)-\ell}{\tau} - C_1\mu_v - C_2\mu_t \quad (25)$$

$$\text{s.t.} \quad \tau = \begin{cases} \frac{1}{\mu_v - \lambda_v^{det}} + \frac{1}{\mu_t - \left[(1-\frac{S-\ell}{r-\ell})(1-\alpha)\lambda_v(S)+\lambda_t\right]} + T, & S < r, \\ \frac{1}{\mu_t - \lambda_t} + T, & S \geq r, \end{cases} \quad (26)$$

$$\lambda_v^{\text{det}} = \lambda_v(1-\alpha) + \lambda_v C_m \alpha \quad (27)$$

$$\mu_v > \lambda_v^{det} \quad (28)$$

$$\mu_t > \beta(S)(1-\alpha)\lambda_v(S) + \lambda_t \tag{29}$$

$$\mu_v \leq \mu_v^{\max} \tag{30}$$

$$\mu_t \leq \mu_t^{\max} \tag{31}$$

$$0 \leq \alpha \leq 1 \tag{32}$$

$$\beta(S) = \begin{cases} 1 - \frac{S-\ell}{r-\ell} & \text{if } S < r \\ 0 & \text{if } S \geq r \end{cases}, \tag{33}$$

$$\lambda_v(S) = \begin{cases} \lambda_v, & S < r \\ 0, & S \geq r \end{cases} \tag{34}$$

$$\mu_v, \mu_t \geq 0 \tag{35}$$

From a queueing perspective, this formulation enforces stage-level stability under work-conserving operation; standard performance measures are monotone in service capacity, so allocating additional feasible capacity to a congested stage improves or at worst does not worsen delay. These properties are standard for single- and multi-server queues and tandem systems [168] [169]. Unlike the costless baseline where total capacity bind, positive capacity costs introduce a principled trade-off: beyond a point, the marginal delay reduction no longer justifies the marginal computational expense, and optimal solutions may rationally leave slack or operate at hardware caps [170]. In interior optima, the allocation equalizes marginal performance gains with the corresponding cost coefficients; at boundaries, the active cap identifies the operative bottleneck [168, 169]. Practically, these principles operate under hard platform limits. The upper bounds imposed on μ_v and μ_t in constraints (30) and (31), respectively, reflect hardware or architectural limitations on processing capabilities. The resulting optimization model is a nonlinear program with linear and piecewise-defined constraints. The objective function is concave, as demonstrated in Appendix E.

Lemma 2. Following the earlier formulation of queueing model, we now derive the optimal service rates μ_v^* and μ_t^* for the detection station v and decision-making station t, respectively. The derived optimal service rates, adjusted to respect the constraints, are:

$$\mu_v^* = \begin{cases} \lambda_v[(1-\alpha)+C_m\alpha]+\Delta_v(S), & S<r,\ 0<\rho(S)<1, \\ & \Delta_v(S)\le U_v,\ \Delta_t(S)\le U_t \\ \lambda_v[(1-\alpha)+C_m\alpha]+\min\left\{\max\left(\frac{\sqrt{\frac{S-\ell}{SC_1}}-1}{K_t},0\right),U_v\right\}, & S<r, \\ & \Delta_t(S)>U_t,\ \Delta_v(S)\le U_v \\ \mu_v^{\max}, & S<r,\ \Delta_v(S)>U_v \\ \lambda_v[(1-\alpha)+C_m\alpha], & S<r, \\ & \rho(S)\ge 1 \text{ or } \Delta_v(S)\le 0 \text{ or } \Delta_t(S)\le 0 \\ 0, & S\ge r\,. \end{cases} \tag{36}$$

$$\mu_t^* = \begin{cases} \lambda_t+\left(1-\frac{S-\ell}{r-\ell}\right)(1-\alpha)\lambda_v+\Delta_t(S), & S<r,\ 0<\rho(S)<1, \\ & \Delta_v(S)\le U_v,\ \Delta_t(S)\le U_t \\ \lambda_t+\left(1-\frac{S-\ell}{r-\ell}\right)(1-\alpha)\lambda_v+\min\left\{\max\left(\frac{\sqrt{\frac{S-\ell}{SC_2}}-1}{T+\frac{1}{U_v}},0\right),U_t\right\}, & S<r, \\ & \Delta_v(S)>U_v,\ \Delta_t(S)\le U_t \\ \mu_t^{\max}, & S<r,\ \Delta_t(S)>U_t \\ \lambda_t+\left(1-\frac{S-\ell}{r-\ell}\right)(1-\alpha)\lambda_v, & S<r, \\ & \rho(S)\ge 1 \text{ or } \Delta_v(S)\le 0 \text{ or } \Delta_t(S)\le 0 \\ \lambda_t+\min\left\{\max\left(\frac{\sqrt{\frac{r-\ell}{SC_2}}-1}{T},0\right),\mu_t^{\max}-\lambda_t\right\}, & S\ge r\,. \end{cases} \tag{37}$$

For $S<r$, $p(S)=\sqrt{\frac{C_1S}{S-\ell}}+\sqrt{\frac{C_2S}{S-\ell}}$, the interior increments $\Delta_v(S)=\frac{1}{T}\sqrt{\frac{S-\ell}{SC_1}}\big(1-p(S)\big)$ and $\Delta_t(S)=\frac{1}{T}\sqrt{\frac{S-\ell}{SC_2}}\big(1-p(S)\big)$, the cap headrooms $U_v=\mu_v^{\max}-\lambda_v\big[(1-\alpha)+C_m\alpha\big]$ and $U_t(S,\alpha)=\mu_t^{\max}-\{\lambda_t+(1-\frac{S-\ell}{r-\ell})(1-\alpha)\lambda_v\}$, and the one–cap denominators $K_v=T+\frac{1}{U_v}$ and $K_t(S,\alpha)=T+\frac{1}{U_t(S,\alpha)}$. For $S\ge r$, we enforce $\mu_v^*=0$ and use the decision-stage headroom $U_t^{(\ge)}=\mu_t^{\max}-\lambda_t$.

Proof of lemma 2 is provided in Appendix F.

4 Numerical Analysis

This chapter presents the results of a series of numerical experiments conducted to investigate the performance characteristics of our two optimization models. The core objective of this investigation is to quantify the sensitivity of five key output metrics to variations in model-specific design parameters and external traffic inputs. The primary dependent variables utilized in this performance analysis are the optimal service rate at detection μ_v^*, the optimal service rate at decision μ_t^*, the overall vehicle flow Q, the total system delay τ, and the average vehicle speed V. The experimental design incorporates two categories of independent variables: those representing design choices controllable by a system architect, and external inputs derived from the traffic stream itself. For the FCC model, the primary design variable under consideration is the total on-board capacity C. In the CAC model, the controllable design parameters are the individual stage capacity limits for detection $\mu_v^{\max}$ and decision $\mu_t^{\max}$. The external inputs, which are varied to simulate diverse operational scenarios, include the arrival rate for detection data λ_v, the arrival rate for decision data λ_t, and the amplification factor C_m. Unless a figure says otherwise, we set $\alpha = 0.5$ and keep the physical interaction parameters at their baseline values. The full set of baseline numbers is listed in Table 1. We assume a connected vehicle environment in which vehicles receive a continuous stream of V2V data. Not all incoming messages necessitate action; rather, only a fraction influence the generation of control commands. We model this by setting the detection-stage arrival rate to $\lambda_v = 0.5$ [work/s], representing the arrival of one impactful message every two seconds, i.e., a message that alters or updates a control decision. Here, work/s represents an abstract processing rate that quantifies the number of meaningful computational tasks completed per second. Each work corresponds to the processing of one relevant or influential message, i.e., a data item that alters the vehicle's situational understanding or control command. This unit is used as a normalized measure of computational throughput across detection and decision stages, independent of hardware or message format. This filtered rate excludes routine or redundant inputs and focuses on those that introduce new context requiring a system-level response. Conversely, the decision/control-related arrival rate is set to

$\lambda_t = 2.5$ [work/s], reflecting the need for more frequent updates in the control stage to maintain smooth and responsive vehicle operation. This ratio (5:1) captures the asymmetry between detection and actuation demands, and supports the modeling of realistic CAV environments where most cooperative or autonomous driving decisions require high-frequency input aggregation and response.

Notation	**Interpretation**	**Default value**
C	Total computational capacity (FCC)	5 [work/s]
C_1	Cost coefficient for μ_v	0.002
C_2	Cost coefficient for μ_t	0.04
ℓ	Safety buffer distance	5 [m]
r	Cooperative/communication range	50 [m]
T	Fixed actuation time	1 [s]
λ_v	Arrival rate at detection stage	0.5 [work/s]
λ_t	Arrival rate at decision stage	2.5 [work/s]
α	Share of malicious data	0.5
C_m	Detection amplification factor	4.0
$\mu_v^{\max}$	Detection service cap (CAC)	3.0 [work/s]
$\mu_t^{\max}$	Decision service cap (CAC)	6.0 [work/s]

Table 1: Parameters used in the numerical experiments.

Hereafter, each subsection presents a sensitivity analysis with respect to the parameter named in its title.

4.1 Ratio of Malicious Data α

This section examines how changes in α shapes optimal service allocations and macroscopic performance within the FCC model. All parameters other than α are held at their default values, and α is varied over representative levels (0.1, 0.5, 0.9). For each density level $k = 1/S$, the closed-form optimizer returns the pair of service rates that satisfy the capacity budget while maximizing flow efficiency. The resulting allocations are then used to evaluate the end-to-end delay, flow, and speed. We also use a finer S-grid near the cooperative-range threshold $(S = r)$ to capture the regime shift: for $S \geq r$ the detection station is deliberately idled and capacity is reallocated to the decision-making stage, producing a distinct change in slope.

Starting with detection allocation μ_v^* in Figure 3(a), at very low density the spacing exceeds the range, so cooperation is inactive and detection idles at $\mu_v^* = 0$. Near $K \approx 1/r$ the regime switches to $K > \frac{1}{r}$ and the interaction term turns on. This change in the active conditions produces a clear kink and a short nonlinear adjustment in μ_v. Deeper in the cooperative range the pattern of active constraints stabilizes and μ_v^* evolves smoothly and is close to linear in K. Larger α raises the effective detection load λ_v^{det}. The optimizer responds by lifting μ_v across the cooperative densities and by shortening the short transition just after the switch.

Turning to decision allocation μ_t^* in Figure 3(b) When $K \leq \frac{1}{r}$ only the decision stage operates, so μ_t^* sits high with ample headroom. At $K \approx \frac{1}{r}$ cooperation activates and the optimal split changes. This produces a step down and a brief nonlinear adjustment. Beyond that short region the same set of constraints remains in force and μ_t^* declines smoothly with K. Higher α shifts more work to detection, so the decision stage carries less effective value from additional service. As a result the μ_t^* curves sit lower for larger α and their high-density tails level off near the lowest stable values.

In Figure 3(c) for a given density K, τ increases with α. A transition is observed near $K \approx$ 20–25 veh/km, where τ shows a discrete increase, most pronounced for $\alpha = 0.9$. Beyond this point, the curves rise gradually and tend to flatten, indicating that additional density produces incremental changes once interactions dominate. These patterns imply that higher α induces greater vehicle-level delay.

Turning to flow, Figure 3(d) shows that Q increases with density until the system enters the cooperative region around $K \approx 20$–25 veh/km; at this point, the added coordination delay becomes binding and Q exhibits a pronounced downward drop. Across the density range, the ordering is consistent: $Q_{\alpha=0.1} > Q_{\alpha=0.5} > Q_{\alpha=0.9}$. Consequently, $\alpha = 0.9$ yields both the lowest peak and the weakest values along the descending branch. The post-peak decline is driven by elevated delay in the cooperative region, which lowers discharge rates.

Regarding the speed, Figure 3(e) shows an analogous effect. V declines with density and displays a marked drop at the entry into the cooperative region ($K \approx 20$–25 veh/km). This drop reflects the same mechanism: once cooperative constraints impose additional delay, realized speeds fall.

Across essentially all relevant densities, the curves are ordered $V_{\alpha=0.1} > V_{\alpha=0.5} > V_{\alpha=0.9}$, indicating that higher α amplifies delay and thus lowers speeds.

Overall, increasing the attack share α increases delay, which not only reduces flow Q and speed V at a given density but also precipitates an earlier and more pronounced downward drop in both quantities upon entry into the cooperative region, reflecting the binding effect of coordination-induced delay. After this transition, the descending branches remain depressed as α rises; consequently, $\alpha = 0.9$ performs worst, $\alpha = 0.5$ is intermediate, and $\alpha = 0.1$ performs best across the examined densities.

We now describe the behavior shown in the five sensitivity plots for the CAC model, computed using the KKT closed-form allocations, displayed in Figure 4, where the three curves correspond to $\alpha \in \{0.1, 0.5, 0.9\}$.

The allocation panels reveal a consistent rebalancing of compute as density grows. In Figure 4(a), the optimal detection rate μ_v^* is zero for the regime where the distance exceeds the cooperative range ($S \geq r$, i.e., $K \leq \frac{1}{r}$); in that region the vehicle has no neighbors to screen and the detection stage is idle by design, so the three α-curves coincide. Once density crosses the threshold of the cooperative range ($K > 1/r$), μ_v^* jumps to a positive interior solution and then gradually increases to its maximum as the mix of treated traffic increases with both K and α and remains at its upper limit.

Figure 4(b) shows that, outside the cooperative range , μ_t^* increases with density. This rise occurs because traffic-level actions exhibit a coordination-scale effect: as density grows but before cooperative constraints activate, a unit of μ_t shapes a larger set of emerging interactions and network-wide patterns, so its marginal effectiveness increases and the optimizer assigns more weight to μ_t. In the same region, μ_v^* is typically pinned at zero, leaving μ_t as the active lever for further improvement, which explains the relatively high values of μ_t^*. At the entry to the cooperative range, the active optimality conditions switch, producing the observed discrete drop; beyond that point, μ_t^* decreases with density as tighter interactions reduce the incremental effectiveness of additional traffic-level work; moreover, larger α implies that fewer V2V signals pass the filter to the next stage, further

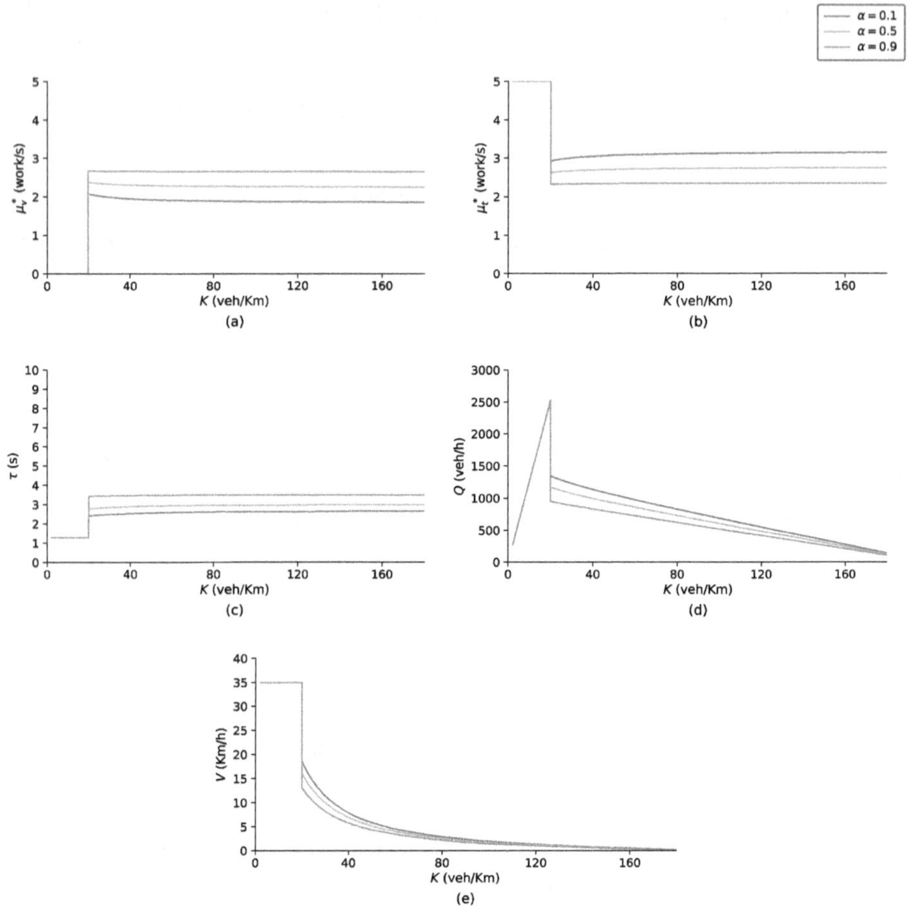

Figure 3: Sensitivity analysis of the FCC model to attack rate α ($\alpha = 0.1, 0.5, 0.9$): (a) μ_v (work/s), (b) μ_t (work/s), (c) τ (s), (d) Q (veh/km), (e) V (km/h).

lowering the value of traffic-level action and shifting μ_t^* downward. Across the range, the ordering is preserved: $\mu_{t,\alpha=0.1}^* > \mu_{t,\alpha=0.5}^* > \mu_{t,\alpha=0.9}^*$.

The end-to-end delay τ in Figure 4(c) increases monotonically with density once $K > 1/r$. The initial kink at $K \approx 20$ veh/km corresponds to the structural switch from the range-limited branch to the two-stage pipeline. For a fixed density, higher α yields larger τ because a greater share of arrivals must traverse the costlier detection path, shrinking available slack in both stages.

Figure 4(d) displays a rise–drop–decay pattern. As density approaches the entry to the cooperative range, flow increases to a local maximum; upon entry, Q exhibits a discrete drop, most visible for $\alpha = 0.9$, after which it declines approximately linearly with K. Increasing α depresses flow across densities:the entire descending branch shifts downward, yielding the ordering $Q_{\alpha=0.1} > Q_{\alpha=0.5} > Q_{\alpha=0.9}$ for K beyond the cooperative threshold.

The speed panel in Figure 4(e) conveys the same effect from a kinematic perspective. Speeds are high and identical across α while $S \geq r$, then drop sharply just after $K \approx 20$ veh/km and continue to fall with density; higher α yields uniformly lower speeds because the detection workload is heavier.

Taken together, the five panels present a coherent picture for the CAC model. Below the cooperative-range threshold all values of α behave the same: detection idles, decision dominates, delays are low, and both speed and flow are high. Beyond that threshold, a larger α shifts the optimal budget toward detection, reduces the decision-stage allocation, increases delay, lowers speed, and suppresses the attainable flow. The visible kink near $K \approx 20$ veh/km is the model's structural transition into cooperation; it marks where interaction begins to shape performance and explains the subsequent trends.

4.2 Total Computationl Capacity

We conduct two complementary sensitivity studies to quantify how compute resources shape cyber–physical traffic performance. First, within the FCC model we vary the total onboard computational capacity C while holding all other parameters fixed, and trace the resulting changes in allocation $\{\mu_v^*, \mu_t^*\}$,flow Q, delay τ, and speed V across density K. Second, within the CAC model we vary the stage–specific caps, detection $\mu_v^{\max}$ and decision $\mu_t^{\max}$, over prescribed grids while keeping remaining inputs constant, again evaluating $\{\mu_v^*, \mu_t^*\}$, Q,τ, and V over K. Together, these experiments isolate the impact of (i) aggregate compute (FCC) and (ii) stage–wise budgets (CAC) on macroscopic traffic outcomes, using consistent units (e.g., Q in veh/h, K in veh/km, τ in s, μ in work/s) and identical density ranges for being comparable.

We begin by examining the FCC model's sensitivity to the total onboard computational capacity,

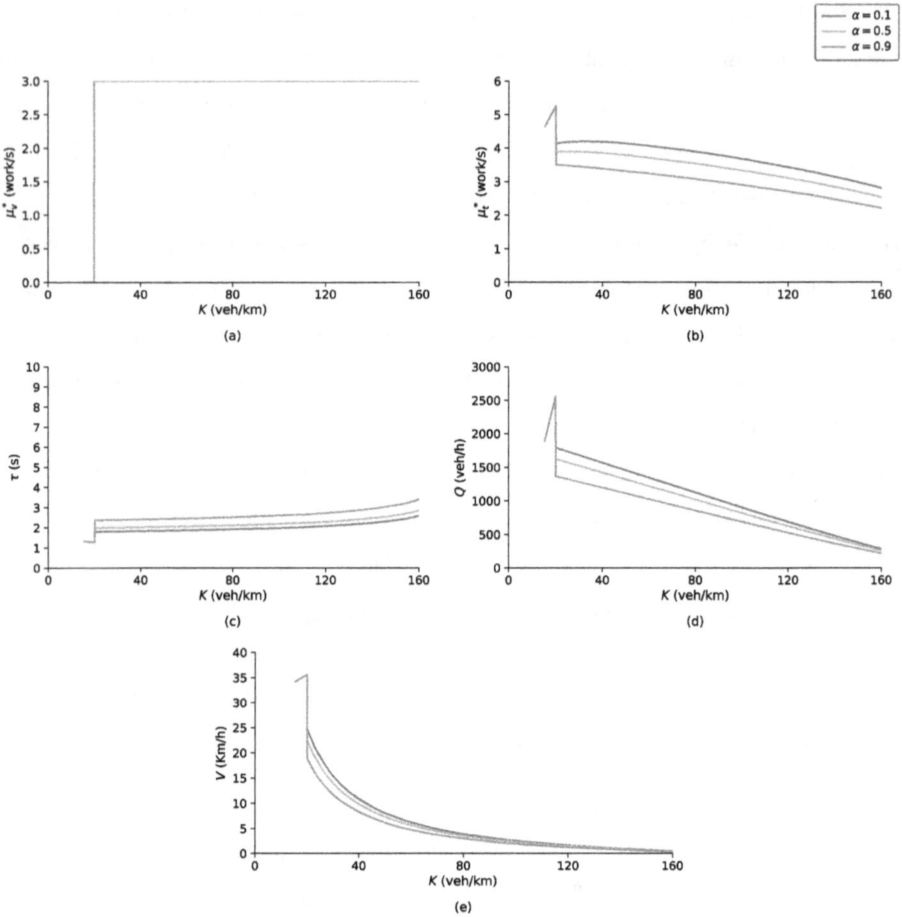

Figure 4: Sensitivity analysis of the CAC model to attack rate α (α = 0.1, 0.5, 0.9): (a) μ_v, (b) μ_t, (c) τ (s), (d) Q (veh/h), (e) V (km/h).

using three capacity settings, 4, 6, and 8 work/s, while keeping the ratio of malicious data fixed at 0.5 and all other parameters at their baseline values. Figure 5 organizes results by capacity across rows, with each curve shown as a function of density; within this layout, the coloumns report the optimal detection rate, the optimal decision rate, the resulting traffic flow, the total processing delay, and the vehicle speed.

Starting with the optimal detection service rate in Figures 5(a), (f) and (k), as total capacity C increases, μ_v^* rises across all densities where cooperation is active. At low densities, when vehicles are spaced far apart and detection demand is light, μ_v^* stays near its baseline. Once cooperation begins, detection work jumps, so μ_v^* increases quickly and then levels off. In the middle, when neither stage is at a hardware limit and the two stages carry comparable burden, the optimizer balances them and the allocation is nearly even: $\mu_v^* \approx C/2$. Exact equality holds only when the effective loads on detection and decision are the same; otherwise the heavier side gets slightly more than half.

The decision rate μ_t^* in Figures 5(b), (g) and (l) follows the complementary pattern. Before cooperation starts, decision handles the whole pipeline, so μ_t^* is high. When detection turns on, μ_t^* drops as capacity shifts to cover the new detection workload. Beyond that point, μ_t^* settles and may drift gently as density grows. In the interior operating region, again, away from caps and with balanced stage demands, the split is essentially even, so $\mu_t^* \approx C/2$. This becomes exact only when the two stages face equal effective load; if decision is lighter or heavier, its share sits a bit below or above half. Increasing C lifts the whole μ_t^* curve since both stages can run faster without pushing delay up elsewhere.

Figures 5(c), (h), and (m) plot total processing delay versus density. At low densities, τ is small and nearly flat. When density reaches the cooperation threshold, τ exhibits a distinct step upward: the detection stage activates and its effective input rises abruptly. Beyond this step, delay increases with K, but the growth depends strongly on total capacity C. With smaller C, τ keeps climbing and becomes more curved at high K, signaling proximity to saturation. As C increases, the entire curve shifts downward and the post-step rise becomes milder, showing that additional capacity both shrinks the jump at the threshold and dampens the subsequent growth of delay across the cooperative range.

These shifts feed directly into traffic performance. Flow trends in Figures 5(d), (i) and (n), follow the familiar concave shape. At low densities, when vehicles are far apart and interaction is minimal, flow rises sharply as cooperation activates and communication between vehicles improves coordination. As density increases from free flow, Q rises to a peak at roughly the same K across all total capacities C. What changes with C is the height of that peak, larger C yields a higher maximum flow. Immediately after the peak there is a sharp step down when cooperation becomes active; this step is smaller when C is larger (the post-peak level starts higher) and larger when C is smaller. Beyond that step, Q follows a nearly linear decline with density; the slope is similar across capacities, but the whole branch is shifted upward when C is higher and downward when C is lower.

Finally Figures 5(e), (j), and (o) illustrate how mean vehicle speed varies with density under different total capacities C. At very low densities, vehicles operate independently with minimal interaction delays, and higher C results in slightly higher free-flow speeds because greater processing capacity reduces baseline latency even before cooperation begins. As density increases and the system enters the cooperative regime ($K \approx 1/r$), all curves exhibit an abrupt drop in speed as communication and detection loads rise sharply. This drop is less severe for larger C, indicating that additional capacity helps absorb the extra processing burden introduced by cooperation. Beyond this transition, V decreases smoothly with increasing K, reflecting the accumulation of delay as spacing tightens. Across the entire range, larger C consistently maintains higher speeds, demonstrating that higher computational capacity mitigates congestion effects by keeping end-to-end delays lower. In the dense regime, all curves eventually approach near-zero speeds, though higher C flattens the tail, delaying full breakdown.

Taken together, Figure 5 shows a coherent mechanism: more total capacity enables a better balance between detection and decision as density grows, which lowers delay, elevates speed, and increases the achievable flow peak. The differences across capacity settings are most pronounced where cooperative processing is most demanding, underscoring that investments in compute pay off most in moderate-to-high density regimes.

Now we turn to the CAC model. We sweep $\alpha = 0.5$ and consider four cap pairs for the two service stages, $(\mu_v^{\max}, \mu_t^{\max}) \in \{(2.5, 5.0), (2.5, 7.0), (3.5, 5.0), (3.5, 7.0)\}$. In Fig 6, the rows correspond to these four cap combinations (top to bottom), while the columns display, from left to right, the

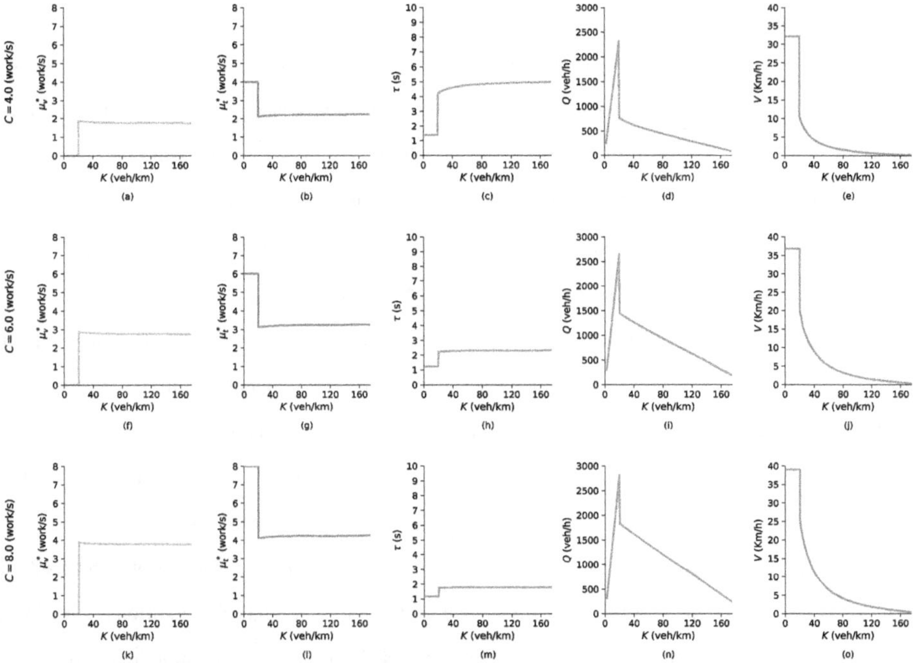

Figure 5: Sensitivity of the FCC model to total computational capacity C ($C = 4, 6, 8$ work/s; $\alpha = 0.5$): (a) μ_v^* (work/s), (b) μ_t^* (work/s), (c) τ (s), (d) Q (veh/h), (e) V (km/h).

detection rate, the decision rate, total delay, flow, and speed. This layout highlights how tightening or relaxing either cap shifts the optimal allocation between detection and decision processes and, in turn, shapes macroscopic traffic outcomes such as delay, flow, and speed.

Across all four configurations, the detection-stage service rate μ_v^* in Figures 6(a), (f), (k) and (p) exhibits a consistent plateau pattern. In each case, μ_v^* rapidly reaches its upper limit at $K = \frac{1}{r}$ and remains constant thereafter, indicating that the detection process operates at full capacity throughout the entire density range. Increasing $\mu_v^{\max}$ shifts the plateau upward, whereas variations in $\mu_t^{\max}$ exert negligible influence, confirming that the detection stage is internally constrained and largely decoupled from the decision-stage capacity. This behavior suggests that the detection component is consistently saturated and does not adapt dynamically to changing traffic density, implying that system-wide performance variations are primarily governed by decision-stage capacity rather than detection-stage limits.

The evolution of total delay τ reflects how cooperative load and computational capacity interact as traffic density increases. At low densities, vehicles operate largely independently, and no cooperative communication occurs. In this regime, the detection process is effectively inactive, while the decision stage handles its limited workload easily within the available capacity, keeping τ nearly constant and small. As K increases and vehicles begin to interact more frequently, computational demand rises sharply, causing the system to enter a cooperative regime. This regime shift appears as the sudden upward jump in τ at boundary of $K = 1/r$. In Figures 6(h) and (r) with a higher $\mu_t^{\max}$ (e.g., 7.0), the decision process can initially absorb the extra demand, resulting in a smoother, earlier rise in delay. In contrast, when $\mu_t^{\max}$ is smaller (e.g., 5.0) in Figures 6(c) and (m), the system retains stable performance for longer but experiences a more abrupt increase once the decision stage saturates. Beyond this transition, τ continues to increase nonlinearly. This curvature occurs because congestion and computational coupling amplify each other: as density grows, the slack in both detection and decision rates decreases, causing the marginal delay per additional vehicle to grow disproportionately. Consequently, the overall trend of τ reflects not a simple linear response to traffic load, but a compound, nonlinear degradation driven by interacting communication and computational constraints.

The flow patterns in Figures 6(d), (i), (n) and (s) further illustrate the effect of computational saturation on macroscopic traffic performance. Before vehicles enter the cooperative range, flow Q increases smoothly as interactions are minimal and each vehicle operates independently. Once cooperation begins, a sudden rise in computational demand causes a sharp drop in Q, marking the transition from individual to coordinated operation. The magnitude of this drop varies with the capacity settings: lower $\mu_t^{\max}$ values produce a more pronounced loss, while higher capacities buffer the effect and yield a smaller discontinuity. Beyond this point, flow decreases almost linearly as density and delay continue to grow, reflecting the progressive impact of computational congestion on throughput.

Vehicle speed shown in Figures 6(e), (j), (o) and (t), starts high in the non-cooperative regime, where vehicles operate independently and delays are minimal. As density increases beyond this range, cooperation activates and processing delays emerge, producing a sharp reduction in speed. This discontinuity mirrors the drop in Q and marks the onset of computational coupling between vehicles. After this transition, V continues to decline smoothly but nonlinearly with increasing K, reflecting the growing impact of communication congestion. The overall level of V depends primarily on the decision-stage capacity: higher $\mu_t^{\max}$ values support slightly higher speeds across all densities, while lower capacities exacerbate the slowdown.

Taken together, the results demonstrate that system performance in the CAC model is shaped predominantly by the available decision-stage capacity. While the detection process rapidly saturates and remains constant, variations in $\mu_t^{\max}$ significantly affect how the system absorbs cooperative workload as density increases. A larger $\mu_t^{\max}$ not only moderates delay growth but also mitigates the abrupt loss in flow and speed at the onset of cooperation, yielding smoother performance across the density range. Conversely, tighter decision caps amplify nonlinear congestion effects, producing steeper rises in delay and sharper drops in macroscopic flow and velocity. Overall, the CAC outcomes reveal that balancing computational resources between detection and decision stages is crucial to sustaining stable traffic operation under cooperative conditions.

4.3 Arrival Rates λ_v and λ_t

Here we investigate sensitivity to the arrival rates that drive the two processing stages. Varying the detection workload and the decision-stage workload allows us to probe how the pipeline reallocates resources and how these shifts propagate to traffic variables. Throughout this analysis the modeling assumptions and plotting conventions follow the earlier sections; only the exogenous arrival rates are perturbed while other parameters remain unchanged for comparability across scenarios. The resulting panels present, for each parameter combination, the optimal stage allocations alongside the induced delay, flow, and speed as functions of density.

We interpret the FCC sensitivity to arrival rates using the Figure 7. The panel set contrasts how optimal allocations and traffic outcomes evolve with density when the detection-arrival rate λ_v and

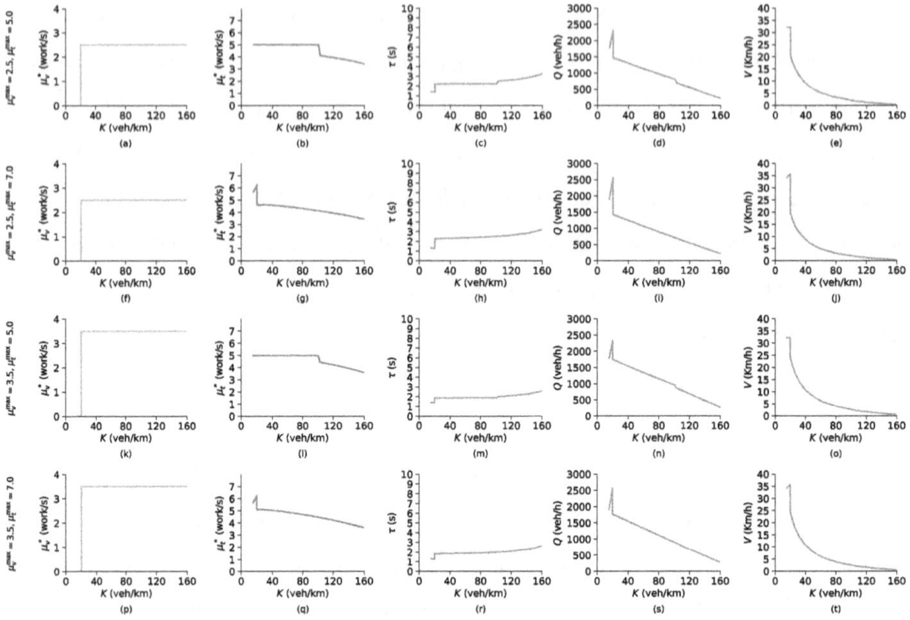

Figure 6: Sensitivity of the CAC model to capacity caps $\mu_v^{\max}$ and $\mu_t^{\max}$: (a) μ_v^* (work/s), (b) μ_t^* (work/s), (c) τ (s), (d) Q (veh/h), (e) V (km/h).

the decision-arrival rate λ_t vary across the rows.

We first compare the allocation panels. The optimal detection rate in 7(a), (f), (k) and (p) rises from zero only after density crosses the cooperation onset. It then jumps to a plateau and remains flat until late in the range. Raising the detection arrival rate lifts this whole plateau, because more detection work must be stabilized as soon as cooperation is active.

In contrast, the optimal decision rate in Figures 7(b), (g), (l) and (q) starts high at light traffic, reflecting that before cooperation turns on, essentially all available capacity can be devoted to decisions. Once cooperation activates, it steps down and then stabilizes. In fact, the decision rate complements the detection rate, as their sum must equal the total system capacity C.

The delay curves in Figures 7(c), (h), (m) and (r) make this asymmetry clear. With a light decision load, delay sits near its floor across a broad density band and grows only gradually. A higher value of λ_t leads to increased delays in the cooperative regime and results in a sharper rise in the delay curve near the transition point.

Those allocation shifts map directly to the traffic outputs. The flow curves show the familiar rapid rise to a single peak followed by a long, nearly linear descent. Heavier detection arrivals lower the peak modestly, because more capacity is tied up in detection as soon as cooperation begins. Heavier decision arrivals in Figures 7(n) and (s) have a stronger effect. The peak flow drops further, which is consistent with the decision stage retaining more of the budget and leaving less slack overall.

The speed panels in Figures 7(e), (j), (o) and (t) complete the picture. Higher arrivals of either type pull the curve downward, and the degradation is sharper when the decision arrivals are high, matching what is seen in delay and flow.

Looking across rows reinforces these interpretations. Raising only detection arrivals primarily elevates detection allocation and mildly degrades throughput, while the shapes of decision, delay, and speed change only modestly. Raising the decision arrival rate increases delay in the cooperative regime and results in a sharper rise at higher densities, while also reducing the overall flow.

Now we examine the CAC model under four arrival rate settings for detection and decision tasks, with $\alpha = 0.5$ and the service caps held fixed across all plots. The rows of the figure correspond to $(\lambda_v, \lambda_t) = (0.75, 2)$, $(1.0, 2)$, $(0.75, 2.5)$, and $(1.0, 2.5)$ (work/s), and the columns show, from left to right, the optimal detection rate μ_v^*, the optimal decision rate μ_t^*, the total processing delay τ, the resulting flow Q, and the speed V, each as a function of density K.

Beginning with the optimal detection allocation, we observe that all four combinations of arrival rates produce a long nearly horizontal plateau at about 3 work/s across the cooperative density range. This uniform cap like behavior shows that detection is constrained by its available service cap rather than by demand. Raising the detection arrival rate from 0.75 to 1.0 does not increase the plateau because the solution is already saturating the detection limit. The decision arrival rate influences only the extreme high density end of the curves.

Across all four arrival–rate configurations in Figures 8(b), (g), (l) and (q), the optimal decision service rate μ_t^* displays a consistent piecewise behavior. Initially, in the free-flow regime, the controller allocates decision service at or near the cap, reflecting low computational strain. Upon

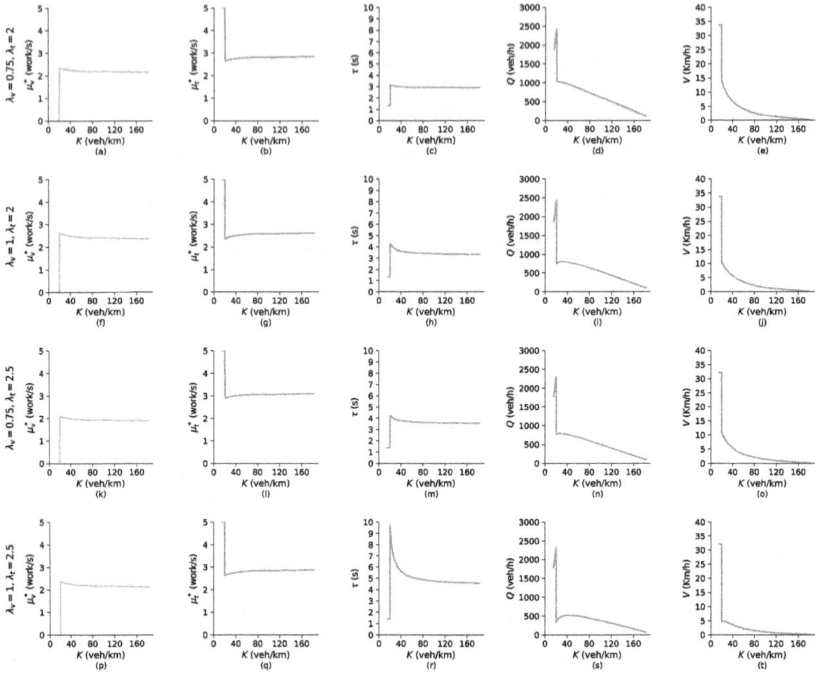

Figure 7: Sensitivity of the FCC model to arrival rates (λ_v, λ_t) ($(\lambda_v, \lambda_t) = (0.75, 2), (1.0, 2.5)$; $\alpha = 0.5, C = 5$ work/s): (a) μ_v^* (work/s), (b) μ_t^* (work/s), (c) τ (s), (d) Q (veh/h), (e) V (km/h).

entering the cooperative regime, when vehicles begin to interact, a sharp drop occurs, followed by a steady decline with increasing density. Increasing the decision arrival rate λ_t from 2.0 to 2.5 [work/s] elevates the entire μ_t^* profile, indicating that the system maintains a higher decision processing effort to accommodate the higher load. Meanwhile, increasing the detection arrival rate λ_v from 0.75 to 1.0 [work/s] shifts the drop in μ_t^* to occur slightly later in density, as more computational effort will be redirected toward decision stage. This dynamic reflects the internal resource balancing of the system in response to changing cyber–physical demands.

The delay curves in Figures 8(c), (h), (m), and (r) rise monotonically with density and share two features across settings. First, a small step appears when cooperation activates at low densities, after which delay stays near a low baseline before increasing. Second, the detection–stage arrival rate controls how quickly delay departs that baseline and how steeply it grows at higher densities.

A higher detection load extends the low-delay window and causes a later, sharper upswing that reaches the largest values at high densities. Changes in the decision arrival rate ($\lambda_t = 2$ to 2.5) are secondary: they shift the curves slightly upward and bring forward the onset of growth, but the effect is modest compared with λ_v. Overall, delay is much more sensitive to the detection workload, while decision mainly adds a small upward bias.

Across all four parameter combinations shown in Figures 8(d), (i), (n), and (s), the flow–density relationship exhibits the characteristic triangular shape with a sharp peak at the cooperative threshold followed by a linear decline as vehicle density increases. Raising the arrival rates do not change the peak but increasing the detection arrival rate λ_v from 0.75 to 1.0 work/s cause the drop be more significant, but increasing the decision arrival rate λ_t shifts the profile upward cause more resources will be allocated to decision station. Then the flow degrade linearly beyond the drop, highlighting a trade-off between performance and robustness under load.

Finally, in the speed Figures 8(e), (j), (o), and (t), velocity falls monotonically with density and the whole plot shifts downward as arrivals increase. Raising either arrival rate depresses the whole curve, but the effect is markedly stronger for the detection workload: with $\lambda_v = 1$ the drop appears larger and the subsequent decay is steeper, mirroring the larger delay observed in the corresponding rows. Changes in the decision arrival rate have a milder influence, mainly nudging the curves downward without substantially altering their shape. Taken together, these trends indicate that, under the CAC policy, macroscopic traffic speed is most sensitive to the detection-stage burden, while decision demand plays a secondary role.

4.4 Detection Amplification Factor C_m

The allocation patterns in Figures 9(a), (b), (f), (g), (k) and (l) show that the optimal detection rate μ_v^* increases with the amplification factor C_m, while the corresponding decision allocation μ_t^* decreases. Across different C_m values, the levels at which the allocations settle after the drop are distinct. In other words, the decline always begins at the same density, yet the point where the curve stabilizes on the y–axis shifts with C_m, reflecting the altered balance between detection and

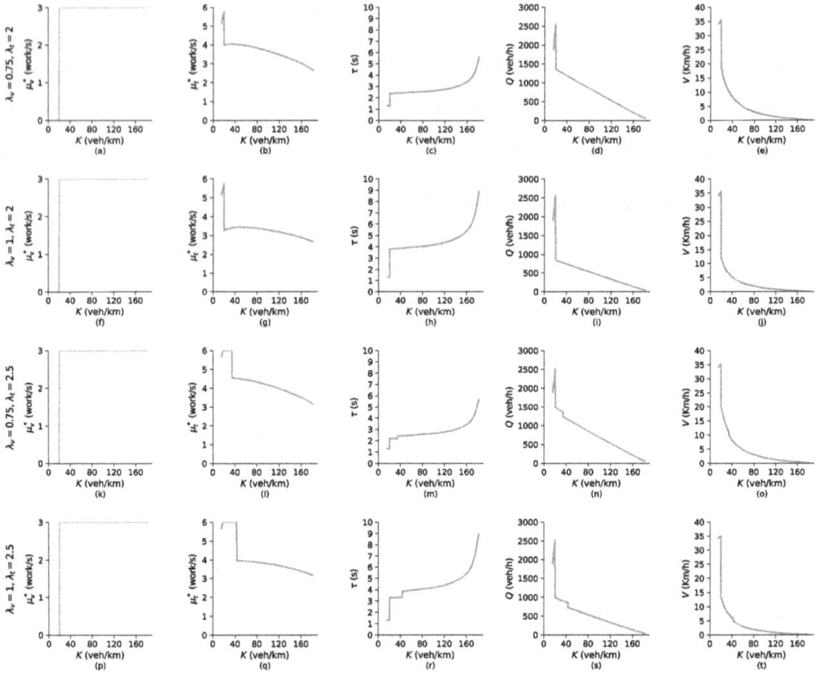

Figure 8: Sensitivity of CAC model to arrival rates Sensitivity of the CAC model to arrival rates (λ_v, λ_t) ($(\lambda_v, \lambda_t) = \{(0.75, 2), (1.0, 2), (0.75, 2.5), (1.0, 2.5)\}$; $\alpha = 0.5$, $C = 6$ work/s): (a) μ_v^* (work/s), (b) μ_t^* (work/s), (c) τ (s), (d) Q (veh/h), (e) V (km/h).

decision capacity.

The delay results in Figures 9 (c), (h) and (m) reveal the same mechanism. With small C_m, delay rises gradually and stabilizes at a relatively low ceiling. As C_m increases, the delay still begins to rise at the same density, but the final values after the growth are higher. This indicates that amplification does not alter when congestion sets in but raises the asymptotic congestion burden once the system saturates.

Turning to the traffic performance, Figures 9(d), (i) and (n) demonstrate that flow follows the familiar single–peaked pattern: it rises sharply before declining almost linearly. The maximum peak is nearly unchanged across the scenarios, but higher C_m shifts the point where the decline stops, leading to different flow levels at high density. This shows that amplification does not expand throughput but modifies the long–run equilibrium level of service.

Finally, the velocity profiles in Figures 9(e), (j) and (o) mirror the flow and delay outcomes. The initial drop in speed occurs at the same point across all scenarios, yet the eventual stabilized speeds differ depending on C_m. Higher amplification lowers the final stable velocity, confirming that stronger detection effort reshapes the end state of the system rather than the onset of its decline.

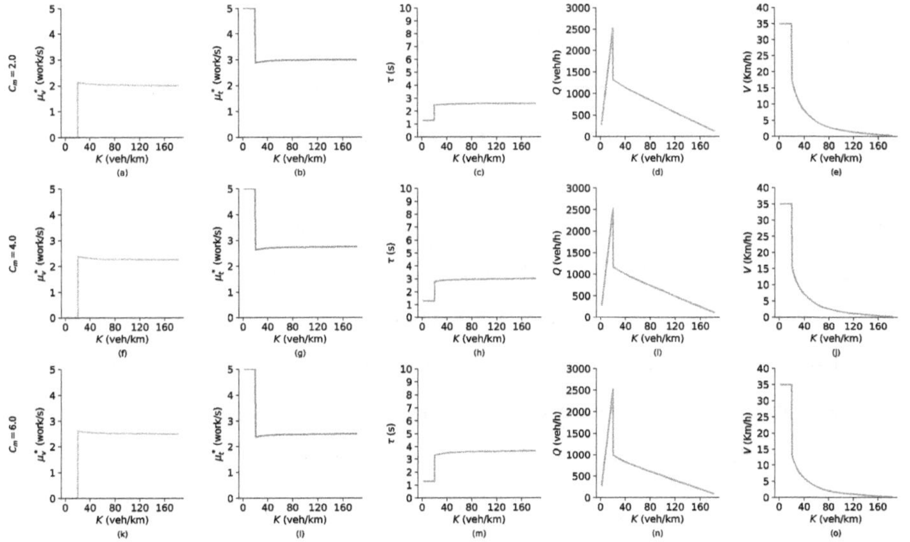

Figure 9: Sensitivity of the FCC model to the detection amplification factor C_m ($C_m = 2.0, 4.0, 6.0$): (a) μ_v^* (work/s), (b) μ_t^* (work/s), (c) τ (s), (d) Q (veh/h), (e) V (km/h).

In Figures 10(c), (h), (m) and (r), the detection allocation μ_v^* is essentially flat at the cap $\mu_v^{\max} \approx 3$ across the cooperative density range for all three amplification levels $C_m \in \{2, 4, 6\}$. What differs is the tail behavior at very high density. For moderate C_m (e.g., 2 or 4), μ_v^* shows a small late-density decline after a long cap-bound stretch, whereas for larger $C_m = 6$ the curve stays pinned at the cap with no drop. The reason is that at high K the optimality region shifts. The decision stage becomes the tight side of the pipeline, and the KKT conditions no longer justify keeping detection fully saturated. So, if there is any slack on detection, the optimizer backs μ_v^* off the cap to reduce end-to-end delay. When C_m is large, the treated detection load λ_v^{det} is so high that detection must remain cap-limited for stability, leaving no room for that late decline.

Turning to decision allocation in Figures 10(b), (g), and (l), at low density the spacing S exceeds the range r, so cooperation is inactive and only the decision stage operates. In this regime extra decision capacity directly reduces delay, and the optimizer selects a high μ_t^* close to its feasible level. The small spike near the left edge marks the switch into the cooperative regime as S drops below r. Once cooperation is active and density grows, μ_t^* declines smoothly. Two forces drive this pattern: (i) the geometric factor $\frac{\min(S,r)-\ell}{S}$ compresses as vehicles get closer, limiting the flow benefit unlocked by faster processing; and (ii) the detection workload rises with interaction, so detection delay becomes the dominant contributor to end-to-end latency. Under CAC there is a cost for decision capacity and no shared budget with detection; therefore the marginal value of increasing μ_t diminishes, and the optimum runs decision with only a modest headroom above its required load, hence the gentle downward slope of μ_t^* with K. At high density the decline continues because the effective bottleneck is upstream at detection and the geometry is unfavorable. Raising μ_t then has little leverage on total delay while still incurring cost, so the controller backs off toward the lowest stable value, producing the low tails on the right of 10(b), (g), and (l). The amplification factor C_m shifts the entire relationship: larger C_m inflates the fraction of messages that must be vetted, making detection dominant earlier and more strongly. Consequently the μ_t^* curves sit lower across densities and end at smaller high-density values. Smaller C_m leaves more room for decision speed to influence delay, so the curves remain higher throughout.

The delay results in Figures 10(c), (h) and (m) show that each curve exhibits a small step up right at the cooperation threshold ($K \approx 1/r$), where the regime switches from $S \geq r$ to $S < r$. At that point the detection stage turns on and its effective arrival jumps to λ_v^{det}, so τ rises abruptly. Moving across densities, delay then grows gradually and becomes more convex at high K as the decision stage operates closer to its cap, making extra load translate into disproportionately larger waiting time. Across rows the larger amplification factor C_m from (d) to (i) to (n) lifts the entire curve. It raises the post step baseline and steepens the late density surge because the heavier detection workload leaves less headroom throughout the cooperative range.

In panels 10(d), (i), and (n) the flow Q rises steeply at low density and attains its peak at the onset of cooperation (near $K \approx 1/r$). Immediately after that point there is a sharp drop from the peak to the start of the long, almost–linear descending branch. As the amplification factor increases from $C_m = 2$ to $C_m = 4$ to $C_m = 6$, this instantaneous drop is larger and, equivalently, the level at which the linear branch begins is lower. Mechanistically, larger C_m increases the effective detection load λ_v^{det}; when the regime switches to $S < r$, the detector's workload jumps while $\mu_v^{\max}$ is unchanged, so delay increases abruptly and the attainable flow falls more. Beyond that step, the decline with K remains close to linear and has a similar slope across the three cases; the curves are mainly shifted downward for larger C_m because the pipeline carries a heavier detection burden throughout the cooperative range.

Finally, in Figures 10(e), (j) and (o) , speed drops sharply at $K \approx 1/r$ and then decreases monotonically with density. Looking across C_m, higher amplification pushes the whole curve downward because the larger detection load elevates τ at every density, so vehicles sustain lower speeds for the same K. Toward the congested end, the tails approach zero more quickly when C_m is larger, reflecting the sharper late-density growth in τ under heavier detection amplification.

Overall, the C_m sweep for the CAC model points to a single mechanism that drives every panel in

Figure 10. Larger C_m raises the effective detection arrivals, so the optimizer keeps detection at its cap across most of the cooperative range and lets the decision rate taper with density because added decision service brings less delay relief while detection dominates. At the onset of cooperation the curves step from the free–range branch to the cooperative branch, and this step becomes more severe as C_m grows. Flow then sits on a lower linear–looking track, delay runs higher with a steeper high–density rise, and speed drops in parallel. The practical takeaway is direct. Curbing amplification upstream or provisioning more detection capacity yields the greatest improvement, while increasing decision capacity alone cannot recover performance when amplification is heavy at moderate and high densities.

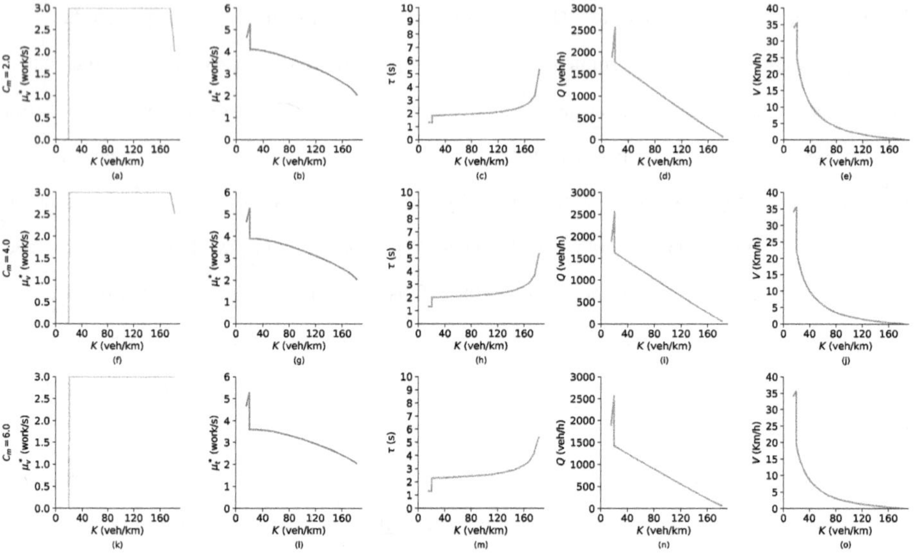

Figure 10: Sensitivity of the CAC model to the detection amplification factor C_m ($C_m = 2.0, 4.0, 6.0$): (a) μ_v^* (work/s), (b) μ_t^* (work/s), (c) τ (s), (d) Q (veh/h), (e) V (km/h).

5 Conclusion

This thesis studied how application-layer flooding attack in V2V communication CAV's control pipeline and ultimately affects macroscopic traffic performance. We modeled the on-board processing chain as a two-stage queue in which the first stage performs detection through the screening of incoming V2V messages and the second stage performs decision-making by executing control computations on sensor and V2I inputs together with filtered V2V data. To evaluate system performance, we considered two optimization models for allocating computational resources across these stages. The first is an FCC model that optimally splits a fixed compute budget C between the two stages. The second is a CAC model that enforces stage-specific caps $\mu_v^{\max}$ and $\mu_t^{\max}$. For each density K closed-form solutions based on the KKT conditions provide the optimal service rates μ_v^* and μ_t^*. These values drive end-to-end delay τ, flow Q, and speed V through a macroscopic mapping that accounts for cooperative range r, safety buffer ℓ, and a fixed actuation overhead T. The attack enters through the malicious share α, the external arrival rates (λ_v, λ_t), and the amplification factor C_m, which captures the additional processing burden on detection stage.

5.1 Key Findings

Four robust patterns emerged across all numerical experiments. First, we characterized the distinct roles and bottlenecks of the two stages. Detection often operates at a broad service rate plateau once cooperation activates, whereas the decision stage begins at a high service rate under light traffic and then tapers as density increases. In both the FCC and CAC models, the decision stage is typically the effective bottleneck at moderate-to-high densities; specifically, raising λ_t narrows the low-delay operating window, depresses the peak flow, shifts the speed knee leftward, and steepens the high-density tail. Second, we analyzed the impact of adversarial load α. A larger α consistently redirects optimal capacity toward the detection stage, raises the total system delay τ for all densities K, and pushes the flow peak Q downward. Also, the visible kink in performance at $K \approx 1/r$ and is a structural feature, indicating the switch to two-stage processing. Third, we examined the effects of compute provisioning. Increasing the total budget C in the FCC model or relaxing the stage caps $\mu_v^{\max}, \mu_t^{\max}$ in the CAC model lifts the feasible service rate plateaus, delays the onset of instability, and increases the peak flow. Performance gains are concentrated in the density regime where cooperation is active, with $\mu_t^{\max}$ showing the strongest leverage on throughput and delay once detection is no longer the binding constraint. Fourth, we assessed arrival rates and coupling. Heavier arrival rate λ_t has a stronger adverse impact than a heavier λ_v, consistently reducing the flow peak Q and advancing the growth of delay. A larger amplification factor C_m exacerbates this asymmetry and makes the capacity reallocation at the cooperation boundary sharper, thereby widening the performance gaps between light and heavy load scenarios.

Collectively, these findings confirm that delay formation under application-layer flooding attacks is fundamentally driven by internal computational bottlenecks within the CAV processing pipeline, rather than by communication latency alone. By integrating delay analysis with a two-stage queuing representation of detection and decision-making, the results show how adversarial V2V traffic reallocates computational capacity across stages, triggers structural regime shifts at the cooperation boundary, and propagates micro-level processing delays into macroscopic traffic performance degradation. This integrated perspective clarifies the mechanisms through which cyber-induced message loads translate into reduced vehicle responsiveness, lower throughput, and altered speed–density relationships.

Moreover these technical findings have implications that extend beyond model behavior and numerical performance, motivating consideration of how such delay mechanisms should be addressed in system design and policy frameworks. From a practical and policy perspective, these findings are particularly relevant for vehicle manufacturers, transportation agencies, and standards and regulatory bodies involved in the deployment of CAVs. For manufacturers and system designers, the results highlight the importance of explicitly accounting for in-vehicle computational bottlenecks when designing detection and decision-making architectures, especially under adversarial communication loads. For transportation authorities and infrastructure operators, the analysis demonstrates that traffic performance degradation under cyberattack can emerge even when physical communication channels remain functional, underscoring the need for cybersecurity-aware performance assessment in cooperative driving applications.

At the policy level, the results support the development of guidelines that go beyond communication reliability and incorporate processing-capacity requirements for cyber-resilient CAV operation. In particular, the findings suggest that standards for V2V-enabled systems should consider minimum processing margins, stage-specific capacity allocation principles, and explicit trade-offs between detection effort and control responsiveness under high message loads. Such considerations can inform future updates to CAV cybersecurity, performance, and interoperability standards, helping ensure that cooperative driving systems maintain safety and throughput in adversarial environments.

5.2 Future Research Directions

This study provides a foundation for understanding the interaction between computational capacity allocation and traffic performance under cyberattacks. However, several promising directions remain open for future investigation. One possible extension is to study mixed traffic settings where CAVs coexist with human-driven vehicles, introducing additional uncertainties in both communication and control. Another important direction is to examine heterogeneous vehicle capabilities, where some CAVs possess stronger sensing, processing, or decision-making resources than others, and to evaluate how these differences affect overall system stability and safety. Incorporating stochastic attack patterns rather than fixed arrival rates could also provide a more realistic representation of cyber–physical threats and enable the design of more robust control strategies. From an application perspective, expanding the framework to network-level analysis instead of a single link would highlight spatial interactions and potential bottlenecks across corridors.

Bibliography

[1] Y. Pan, Y. Wu, L. Xu, C. Xia, and D. L. Olson, "The impacts of connected autonomous vehicles on mixed traffic flow: A comprehensive review," *Physica A: Statistical Mechanics and its Applications*, vol. 635, p. 129454, 2024.

[2] P. Wang, X. Wu, and X. He, "Modeling and analyzing cyberattack effects on connected automated vehicular platoons," *Transportation research part C: emerging technologies*, vol. 115, p. 102625, 2020.

[3] C. Jernberg, J. Sandin, T. Ziemke, and J. Andersson, "The effect of latency, speed and task on remote operation of vehicles," *Transportation Research Interdisciplinary Perspectives*, vol. 26, p. 101152, 2024.

[4] Y. He, H. Chen, and W. Shi, "A faster and more reliable middleware for autonomous driving systems," *arXiv preprint arXiv:2510.11448*, 2025.

[5] Y. Ji, Z. Zhou, Z. Yang, Y. Huang, Y. Zhang, W. Zhang, L. Xiong, and Z. Yu, "Toward autonomous vehicles: A survey on cooperative vehicle-infrastructure system," *Iscience*, vol. 27, no. 5, 2024.

[6] M. S. Sheikh, J. Liang, and W. Wang, "A survey of security services, attacks, and applications for vehicular ad hoc networks (vanets)," *Sensors*, vol. 19, no. 16, p. 3589, 2019.

[7] I. Durlik, T. Miller, E. Kostecka, Z. Zwierzewicz, and A. Lobodzińska, "Cybersecurity in autonomous vehicles—are we ready for the challenge?," *Electronics*, vol. 13, no. 13, p. 2654, 2024.

[8] N. Ahmed, F. Hassan, K. Aurangzeb, A. H. Magsi, and M. Alhussein, "Advanced machine learning approach for dos attack resilience in internet of vehicles security," *Heliyon*, vol. 10, no. 8, 2024.

[9] J. M. Tine, M. Aldeen, A. Enan, M. S. Salek, L. Cheng, and M. Chowdhury, "Real-world evaluation of protocol-compliant denial-of-service attacks on c-v2x-based forward collision warning systems," *arXiv preprint arXiv:2508.02805*, 2025.

[10] Z. PethHo, Z. Szalay, and Á. Török, "Safety risk focused analysis of v2v communication especially considering cyberattack sensitive network performance and vehicle dynamics factors," *Vehicular Communications*, vol. 37, p. 100514, 2022.

[11] Z. Wang, H. Wei, J. Wang, X. Zeng, and Y. Chang, "Security issues and solutions for connected and autonomous vehicles in a sustainable city: A survey," *Sustainability*, vol. 14, no. 19, p. 12409, 2022.

[12] X. Ge, Q.-L. Han, Q. Wu, and X.-M. Zhang, "Resilient and safe platooning control of connected automated vehicles against intermittent denial-of-service attacks," *IEEE/CAA Journal of Automatica Sinica*, vol. 10, no. 5, pp. 1234–1251, 2022.

[13] M. Siracusano, S. Shiaeles, and B. Ghita, "Detection of lddos attacks based on tcp connection parameters," *arXiv preprint arXiv:1904.01508*, 2019.

[14] Q. Xu, L. Zhang, and Y. Liu, "Enhancing trust management system for connected autonomous vehicles using machine learning methods: A survey," *arXiv preprint arXiv:2505.07882*, 2025.

[15] Z. Khattak, H. A. Rakha, and Y. Atallah, "Impact of cyberattacks on safety and stability of connected and automated vehicles," *Accident Analysis & Prevention*, vol. 144, p. 105861, 2020.

[16] L. Zhang, Y. Guo, N. Lu, and D. Yue, "Connected and autonomous vehicles cybersecurity: Challenges and opportunities," *IEEE Internet of Things Journal*, vol. 7, no. 6, pp. 5406–5420, 2020.

[17] I. McManus and K. Heaslip, "The impact of cyberattacks on efficient operations of cavs," *Frontiers in future transportation*, vol. 3, p. 792649, 2022.

[18] J. Guanetti, Y. Kim, and F. Borrelli, "Control of connected and automated vehicles: State of the art and future challenges," *Annual reviews in control*, vol. 45, pp. 18–40, 2018.

[19] H. A. Ignatious, H. El-Sayed, M. A. Khan, and B. M. Mokhtar, "Analyzing factors influencing situation awareness in autonomous vehicles—a survey," *Sensors*, vol. 23, no. 8, p. 4075, 2023.

[20] M. V. Rajasekhar and A. K. Jaswal, "Autonomous vehicles: The future of automobiles," in *2015 IEEE International Transportation Electrification Conference (ITEC)*, pp. 1–6, 2015.

[21] SAE International, "Taxonomy and definitions for terms related to driving automation systems for on-road motor vehicles," sae standard j3016, SAE International, April 2021.

[22] F. Jiménez, *Intelligent Vehicles: Enabling technologies and future developments*. Butterworth-Heinemann, 2017.

[23] P. Patil, "A review of connected and automated vehicle traffic flow models for next-generation intelligent transportation systems," *Appl. Res. Artif. Intell. Cloud Comput*, vol. 1, no. 1, pp. 10–22, 2018.

[24] M. A. Khan, H. E. Sayed, S. Malik, T. Zia, J. Khan, N. Alkaabi, and H. Ignatious, "Level-5 autonomous driving—are we there yet? a review of research literature," *ACM Computing Surveys (CSUR)*, vol. 55, no. 2, pp. 1–38, 2022.

[25] T. Petrov, I. Finkelberg, P. Povcta, L. Buzna, N. Zarkhin, A. Gal-Tzur, and T. Toledo, "An analytical approach to the estimation of vehicular communication reliability for intersection control applications," *Vehicular Communications*, vol. 45, p. 100693, 2024.

[26] X. Huang, D. Zhao, and H. Peng, "Empirical study of dsrc performance based on safety pilot model deployment data," *IEEE Transactions on Intelligent Transportation Systems*, vol. 18, no. 10, pp. 2619–2628, 2017.

[27] O. Kavas-Torris, S. Y. Gelbal, M. R. Cantas, B. Aksun Guvenc, and L. Guvenc, "V2x communication between connected and automated vehicles (cavs) and unmanned aerial vehicles (uavs)," *Sensors*, vol. 22, no. 22, p. 8941, 2022.

[28] D. E. Gettman, "Dsrc and c-v2x: Similarities, differences, and the future of connected vehicles." Kimley-Horn, Perspectives, News Insights, June 2020. Smart Mobility and AV/CV Senior Consultant.

[29] C. Urmson, J. Anhalt, D. Bagnell, C. Baker, R. Bittner, M. Clark, J. Dolan, D. Duggins, T. Galatali, C. Geyer, *et al.*, "Autonomous driving in urban environments: Boss and the urban challenge," *Journal of field Robotics*, vol. 25, no. 8, pp. 425–466, 2008.

[30] J. Santa, A. F. Gómez-Skarmeta, and M. Sánchez-Artigas, "Architecture and evaluation of a unified v2v and v2i communication system based on cellular networks," *computer communications*, vol. 31, no. 12, pp. 2850–2861, 2008.

[31] N. Firdissa, K. A. Gemeda, S. Mishra, D. S. Rathee, R. S. Singh, and T. Darejew, "Disseminating a fair emergency message with v2v communication technology in vanet," *Security and Communication Networks*, vol. 2025, no. 1, p. 8882649, 2025.

[32] National Highway Traffic Safety Administration, "Vehicle-to-vehicle communication technology." `https://www.nhtsa.gov/sites/nhtsa.gov/files/documents/v2v_fact_sheet_101414_v2a.pdf`, 2014. Accessed: 2025-07-25.

[33] J. Zheng, L. Ma, and W. Zhang, "Promotion of driver compliance with v2v information in car-following tasks via multimodal display," *Transportation research part F: traffic psychology and behaviour*, vol. 94, pp. 243–253, 2023.

[34] G. Parikh, M. Duhn, J. Hourdos, *et al.*, "How locals need to prepare for the future of v2v/v2i connected vehicles," tech. rep., Minnesota. Department of Transportation. Research Services & Library, 2019.

[35] U. G. A. Office, "Intelligent transportation systems: Vehicle-to-infrastructure technologies expected to offer benefits, but deployment challenges exist," Tech. Rep. GAO-15-775, U.S. Government Accountability Office, September 2015.

[36] U.S. Department of Transportation, "Evaluation of connected vehicle applications on mahan corridor, phase i," Tech. Rep. FHWA-HRT-23-068, Federal Highway Administration, 2023. Accessed: 2024-06-19.

[37] H. Zhang and L. Du, "Platoon-centered control for eco-driving at signalized intersection built upon hybrid mpc system, online learning and distributed optimization part i: Modeling and solution algorithm design," *Transportation Research Part B: Methodological*, vol. 172, pp. 174–198, 2023.

[38] D. Jia and D. Ngoduy, "Enhanced cooperative car-following traffic model with the combination of v2v and v2i communication," *Transportation Research Part B: Methodological*, vol. 90, pp. 172–191, 2016.

[39] S. A. Yusuf, A. Khan, and R. Souissi, "Vehicle-to-everything (v2x) in the autonomous vehicles domain–a technical review of communication, sensor, and ai technologies for road user safety," *Transportation Research Interdisciplinary Perspectives*, vol. 23, p. 100980, 2024.

[40] National Highway Traffic Safety Administration, "Federal motor vehicle safety standards; v2v communications," tech. rep., National Highway Traffic Safety Administration, 2016. Accessed: 2025-09-02.

[41] T. Ormándi and B. Varga, "The importance of v2x simulation: An in-depth comparison of intersection control algorithms using a high-fidelity communication simulation," *Vehicular Communications*, vol. 44, p. 100676, 2023.

[42] S.-I. Alupoaei and C.-F. Caruntu, "Optimizing urban traffic efficiency and safety via v2x: A simulation study using the mosaic platform," *Sensors*, vol. 25, no. 17, 2025.

[43] E. Charoniti, G. Klunder, P.-P. Schackmann, M. Schreuder, R. de Souza Schwartz, D. Spruijtenburg, U. Stelwagen, and I. Wilmink, "Environmental benefits of c-v2x for 5gaa - 5g automotive association e.v.," Tech. Rep. TNO 2020 R11817, TNO, The Hague, The Netherlands, November 2020. Accessed: 2024-06-19.

[44] H. Hejazi and L. Bokor, "V2x-equipped smart intersections—survey of surveys, use cases, and deployments," *J. Commun*, vol. 18, pp. 722–738, 2023.

[45] National Highway Traffic Safety Administration, "Vehicle-to-vehicle communication technology: Readiness of v2v technology for application," Tech. Rep. Fact Sheet No. 11078-101414-v2a, U.S. Department of Transportation, 2014. Accessed: 2025-07-28.

[46] J. Wang, I. Topilin, A. Feofilova, M. Shao, and Y. Wang, "Cooperative intelligent transport systems: The impact of c-v2x communication technologies on road safety and traffic efficiency," *Sensors (Basel, Switzerland)*, vol. 25, no. 7, p. 2132, 2025.

[47] H. A. Rakha, K. Ahn, J. Du, M. Farag, *et al.*, "Quantifying the impact of cellular vehicle-to-everything (c-v2x) on transportation system efficiency, energy and environment," tech. rep., Urban Mobility & Equity Center, 2023.

[48] K. Jerath, V. V. Gayah, and S. N. Brennan, "Mitigating delay due to capacity drop near freeway bottlenecks: Zones of influence of connected vehicles," *PloS one*, vol. 19, no. 6, p. e0301188, 2024.

[49] L. Cao, H. Yin, J. Hu, and L. Zhang, "Performance analysis and improvement on dsrc application for v2v communication," in *2020 IEEE 92nd Vehicular Technology Conference (VTC2020-Fall)*, pp. 1–6, IEEE, 2020.

[50] Y.-r. Kang, Y. Chen, and C. Tian, "Vehicle-to-vehicle cooperative driving model considering end-to-end delay of communication network," *Scientific reports*, vol. 13, no. 1, p. 22966, 2023.

[51] K. Shah and E. Parentela, "A case study on potential benefits of v2v communication technology on freeway safety," 2015.

[52] X. Shen, J. C. Zhuang, S. Pendleton, W. Liu, B. Qin, G. M. J. Fu, and M. H. Ang, "Multi-vehicle motion coordination using v2v communication," in *2015 IEEE Intelligent Vehicles Symposium (IV)*, pp. 1334–1341, IEEE, 2015.

[53] M. Forster, R. Frank, M. Gerla, and T. Engel, "A cooperative advanced driver assistance system to mitigate vehicular traffic shock waves," in *IEEE Infocom 2014-IEEE Conference on Computer Communications*, pp. 1968–1976, IEEE, 2014.

[54] M. A. Naeem, S. Chaudhary, and Y. Meng, "Road to efficiency: V2v enabled intelligent transportation system," *Electronics*, vol. 13, no. 13, p. 2673, 2024.

[55] Business Wire, "Study shows giving school buses green lights can improve student safety and help address the nation-wide bus driver shortage," October 2022. Accessed: 2024-06-19.

[56] S. E. Shladover, D. Su, and X.-Y. Lu, "Impacts of cooperative adaptive cruise control on freeway traffic flow," *Transportation Research Record*, vol. 2324, no. 1, pp. 63–70, 2012.

[57] L. Xiao, "Cooperative adaptive cruise control vehicles on highways: Modelling and traffic flow characteristics," 2020.

[58] A. Mesdaghi and M. Mollajafari, "Improve performance and energy efficiency of plug-in fuel cell vehicles using connected cars with v2v communication," *Energy Conversion and Management*, vol. 306, p. 118296, 2024.

[59] A. Abdo, S. M. B. Malek, Z. Qian, Q. Zhu, M. Barth, and N. Abu-Ghazaleh, "Application level attacks on connected vehicle protocols," in *22nd International Symposium on Research in Attacks, Intrusions and Defenses (RAID 2019)*, pp. 459–471, 2019.

[60] Q. Dai and L. Shi, "A game-theoretic analysis of cyber attack-mitigation in centralized feeder automation system," in *2020 IEEE Power & Energy Society General Meeting (PESGM)*, pp. 1–5, IEEE, 2020.

[61] H. Mo, X. Xiao, G. Sansavini, and D. Dong, "Optimal defense resource allocation against cyber-attacks in distributed generation systems," *Proceedings of the Institution of Mechanical Engineers, Part O: Journal of Risk and Reliability*, vol. 238, no. 6, pp. 1302–1329, 2024.

[62] L. L. Njilla, C. A. Kamhoua, K. A. Kwiat, P. Hurley, and N. Pissinou, "Cyber security resource allocation: a markov decision process approach," in *2017 IEEE 18th International Symposium on High Assurance Systems Engineering (HASE)*, pp. 49–52, IEEE, 2017.

[63] C. van der Ploeg, J. van de Sluis, S. Gerres, S. Novaczki, A. Wippelhauser, E. Nassor, J. Sevin, A. Gazdag, and G. Biczók, "Secredas: Safe and (cyber-) secure cooperative and automated mobility," *IFAC-PapersOnLine*, vol. 56, no. 2, pp. 7542–7548, 2023.

[64] S. Poochaya, P. Uthansakul, M. Uthansakul, and O. Tonguz, "The improvement of a vehicle to infrastructure communication link for its/dsrc using sdr and mimo technology," *SURANAREE JOURNAL OF SCIENCE AND TECHNOLOGY*, vol. 21, no. 3, pp. 147–161, 2014.

[65] V. A. Aulia, U. K. Usman, and D. Perdana, "Analisa perancangan komunikasi untuk kendaraan dengan infrastruktur (v2i) â€ œanalysis design of vehicle to infrastructure (v2i) communication â€," *eProceedings of Engineering*, vol. 6, no. 1, 2019.

[66] H. Xu, J. Yuan, C. Wang, Y. Shao, A. Berres, and T. Laclair, "A mobile app for intersectional traffic optimization through real-time vehicle-to-infrastructure (v2i) communication and cyber-physical control," in *2022 IEEE 19th International Conference on Mobile Ad Hoc and Smart Systems (MASS)*, pp. 260–261, IEEE, 2022.

[67] G. Lopez-Bernal, A. Jacobi, J. L. Craig, *et al.*, "Transit vehicle-to-infrastructure (v2i) applications: near term research and development: transit vehicle and center data exchange:

operational concept.," tech. rep., United States. Department of Transportation. Intelligent Transportation . . . , 2015.

[68] M. S. Shahriar, A. K. Kale, and K. Chang, "Enhancing intersection traffic safety utilizing v2i communications: Design and evaluation of machine learning based framework," *IEEE Access*, vol. 11, pp. 106024–106036, 2023.

[69] R. Pramoda, A. Kumar, M. Sadiqulla, R. Kumar, and P. Bhuiya, "Smart traffic management system," *International Journal of Advanced Research in Science, Communication and Technology*, 2023.

[70] N. Ekedebe, "On an investigation into intelligent transportation system (its) safety and traffic efficiency applications," in *Mobile Multimedia/Image Processing, Security, and Applications 2015*, vol. 9497, pp. 179–192, SPIE, 2015.

[71] N. M. Mari, S. Arrigoni, F. Braghin, S. Mentasti, and M. Filippini, "A v2i communication framework of adaptive traffic lights and a prototype shuttle," in *2022 AEIT International Annual Conference (AEIT)*, pp. 1–6, IEEE, 2022.

[72] Q. Xiang, L. Kong, X. Chen, Z. Wang, L. Rao, and X. Liu, "Greenbroker: Optimal electric vehicle park-and-charge control via vehicle-to-infrastructure communication," in *2019 IEEE International Black Sea Conference on Communications and Networking (BlackSeaCom)*, pp. 1–5, IEEE, 2019.

[73] S. Chowduri, S. Midlam-Mohler, and K. P. Singh, "Design, prototyping, and implementation of a vehicle-to-infrastructure (v2i) system for eco-approach and departure through connected and smart corridors," tech. rep., SAE Technical Paper, 2024.

[74] S. Diwan, B. Dalla Chiara, and F. Deflorio, "Effect of vehicle and vehicle to infrastructure communication systems on transportation safety," in *Applications of Advanced Technology in Transportation. The Ninth International ConferenceAmerican Society of Civil Engineers*, 2006.

[75] A. R. Khan, M. F. Jamlos, N. Osman, M. I. Ishak, F. Dzaharudin, Y. K. Yeow, and K. A. Khairi, "Dsrc technology in vehicle-to-vehicle (v2v) and vehicle-to-infrastructure (v2i) iot system for intelligent transportation system (its): A review," *Recent trends in mechatronics towards industry 4.0: selected articles from iM3F 2020, Malaysia*, pp. 97–106, 2021.

[76] Y. Wang, Y. Ren, H. Qin, Z. Cui, Y. Zhao, and H. Yu, "A dataset for cyber threat intelligence modeling of connected autonomous vehicles," *Scientific Data*, vol. 12, no. 1, p. 366, 2025.

[77] R. Gesteira-Miñarro, G. López, and R. Palacios, "Revisiting wireless cyberattacks on vehicles," *Sensors*, vol. 25, no. 8, p. 2605, 2025.

[78] A. Giannaros, A. Karras, L. Theodorakopoulos, C. Karras, P. Kranias, N. Schizas, G. Kalogeratos, and D. Tsolis, "Autonomous vehicles: Sophisticated attacks, safety issues, challenges, open topics, blockchain, and future directions," *Journal of Cybersecurity and Privacy*, vol. 3, no. 3, pp. 493–543, 2023.

[79] V. K. Kukkala, S. V. Thiruloga, and S. Pasricha, "Roadmap for cybersecurity in autonomous vehicles," *IEEE Consumer Electronics Magazine*, vol. 11, no. 6, pp. 13–23, 2022.

[80] N. Piperigkos, A. Gkillas, G. Arvanitis, S. Nousias, A. Lalos, A. Fournaris, P. Radoglou-Grammatikis, P. Sarigiannidis, and K. Moustakas, "Distributed intelligence in industrial and automotive cyber–physical systems: a review," *Frontiers in Robotics and AI*, vol. 11, p. 1430740, 2024.

[81] S. A. Ali and S. Din, "Collaborative approaches to enhancing smart vehicle cybersecurity by ai-driven threat detection," *arXiv preprint arXiv:2501.00261*, 2024.

[82] P. K. R. Lebaku, L. Gao, Y. Zhang, Z. Li, Y. Liu, and T. Arafin, "Cybersecurity-focused anomaly detection in connected autonomous vehicles using machine learning," in *International Conference on Transportation and Development 2025*, pp. 566–580, 2025.

[83] R. M. Czekster, "Showcasing standards and approaches for cybersecurity, safety, and privacy issues in connected and autonomous vehicles," *arXiv preprint arXiv:2508.01207*, 2025.

[84] M. Hamad, A. Finkenzeller, M. Kühr, A. Roberts, O. Maennel, V. Prevelakis, and S. Steinhorst, "React: Autonomous intrusion response system for intelligent vehicles," *Computers & Security*, vol. 145, p. 104008, 2024.

[85] W. S. Alaloul, A. H. Qureshi, S. Saad, K. M. Alzubi, and S. Ammad, *Cyber-Physical Systems in the Construction Sector.* CRC Press, 2022.

[86] A. Yousseef, S. Satam, B. S. Latibari, J. Pacheco, S. Salehi, S. Hariri, and P. Satam, "Autonomous vehicle security: A deep dive into threat modeling," *arXiv preprint arXiv:2412.15348*, 2024.

[87] M. De Vincenzi, M. D. Pesé, C. Bodei, I. Matteucci, R. R. Brooks, M. Hasan, A. Saracino, M. Hamad, and S. Steinhorst, "Contextualizing security and privacy of software-defined vehicles: State of the art and industry perspectives," *arXiv preprint arXiv:2411.10612*, 2024.

[88] M. Althunayyan, A. Javed, and O. Rana, "A survey of learning-based intrusion detection systems for in-vehicle network," *arXiv preprint arXiv:2505.11551*, 2025.

[89] M. Scalas and G. Giacinto, "Automotive cybersecurity: Foundations for next-generation vehicles," in *2019 2nd International Conference on new Trends in Computing Sciences (ICTCS)*, pp. 1–6, IEEE, 2019.

[90] A. Beteto, V. Melo, J. Lin, M. Alsultan, E. M. Dias, E. Korte, D. A. Johnson, N. Moghadasi, T. L. Polmateer, and J. H. Lambert, "Anomaly and cyber fraud detection in pipelines and supply chains for liquid fuels," *Environment Systems and Decisions*, vol. 42, no. 2, pp. 306–324, 2022.

[91] S. Ghosh and T. Roy, "Assessment of cyberattack detection-isolation algorithm for cav platoons using sumo," *arXiv preprint arXiv:2503.14628*, 2025.

[92] S. Iqbal, P. Ball, M. H. Kamarudin, and A. Bradley, "Simulating malicious attacks on vanets for connected and autonomous vehicle cybersecurity: A machine learning dataset," in *2022*

13th International Symposium on Communication Systems, Networks and Digital Signal Processing (CSNDSP), pp. 332–337, IEEE, 2022.

[93] J. Janak, *Towards Self-Managing Networked Cyber-Physical Systems*. Columbia University, 2024.

[94] H.-T. Sun, X. Chen, Z. Zhang, X. Ge, and C. Peng, "Data-driven event-triggered sliding mode secure control for autonomous vehicles under actuator attacks," *IEEE Transactions on Cybernetics*, 2024.

[95] W. Almuseelem, "Deep reinforcement learning-enabled computation offloading: A novel framework to energy optimization and security-aware in vehicular edge-cloud computing networks," *Sensors*, vol. 25, no. 7, p. 2039, 2025.

[96] U. Madububa Mbachu, R. Fatima, A. Sherif, E. Dockery, M. Mahmoud, M. Alsabaan, and K. Khalil, "Hardware acceleration-based privacy-aware authentication scheme for internet of vehicles using physical unclonable function," *Sensors*, vol. 25, no. 5, p. 1629, 2025.

[97] M. Talha, E. Ellahi, A. Thirunagalingam, D. Sharath, S. Chundru, and M. Tiwari, "Cyber-physical systems security verification utilising sat-based model checking," in *2024 International Conference on Advances in Computing, Communication and Materials (ICACCM)*, pp. 1–6, IEEE, 2024.

[98] T. Alqubaysi, A. F. Al Asmari, F. Alanazi, A. Almutairi, and A. Armghan, "Federated learning-based predictive traffic management using a contained privacy-preserving scheme for autonomous vehicles," *Sensors (Basel, Switzerland)*, vol. 25, no. 4, p. 1116, 2025.

[99] S. Koppel, D. B. Logan, X. Zou, F. Kaviani, H. McDonald, J. F. Hair Jr, R. M. S. Louis, L. J. Molnar, and J. L. Charlton, "Factors influencing behavioral intentions to use conditionally automated vehicles," *Journal of Safety Research*, vol. 91, pp. 423–430, 2024.

[100] P. Sharma, D. Austin, and H. Liu, "Attacks on machine learning: Adversarial examples in connected and autonomous vehicles," in *2019 IEEE International Symposium on Technologies for Homeland Security (HST)*, pp. 1–7, IEEE, 2019.

[101] K. Grosse and A. Alahi, "A qualitative ai security risk assessment of autonomous vehicles," *Transportation Research Part C: Emerging Technologies*, vol. 169, p. 104797, 2024.

[102] S. Checkoway, D. McCoy, B. Kantor, D. Anderson, H. Shacham, S. Savage, K. Koscher, A. Czeskis, F. Roesner, and T. Kohno, "Comprehensive experimental analyses of automotive attack surfaces," in *20th USENIX security symposium (USENIX Security 11)*, 2011.

[103] X. Sun, F. R. Yu, and P. Zhang, "A survey on cyber-security of connected and autonomous vehicles (cavs)," *IEEE Transactions on Intelligent Transportation Systems*, vol. 23, no. 7, pp. 6240–6259, 2021.

[104] C. Miller and C. Valasek, "Remote exploitation of an unaltered passenger vehicle," *Black Hat USA*, vol. 2015, no. S 91, pp. 1–91, 2015.

[105] SAE International, "Automotive electronics and electrical systems," SAE Technical Paper 2020-01-1236, SAE International, 2020.

[106] I. Mahmoudi, D. E. Boubiche, S. Athmani, H. Toral-Cruz, and F. I. Chan-Puc, "Toward generative ai-based intrusion detection systems for the internet of vehicles (iov)," *Future Internet*, vol. 17, p. 310, July 2025.

[107] J. Petit and S. E. Shladover, "Potential cyberattacks on automated vehicles," *IEEE Transactions on Intelligent transportation systems*, vol. 16, no. 2, pp. 546–556, 2014.

[108] S. Mansfield, J. O'Raw, N. McMurray, and T. McWilliams, "Cybersecurity in the automotive supply chain: Challenges and solutions," *Journal of Automotive Software Engineering*, vol. 1, pp. 1–12, October 2017.

[109] C. O'Flynn and G. d'Eon, "Power analysis and fault attacks against secure can: How safe are your keys?," *SAE International Journal of Transportation Cybersecurity and Privacy*, vol. 1, no. 11-01-01-0001, pp. 3–18, 2018.

[110] R. Hussain and S. Zeadally, "Autonomous cars: Research results, issues, and future challenges," *IEEE Communications Surveys & Tutorials*, vol. 21, no. 2, pp. 1275–1313, 2018.

[111] M. Kühr, M. Hamad, P. MohajerAnsari, M. D. Pesé, and S. Steinhorst, "Sok: Security of the image processing pipeline in autonomous vehicles," *arXiv preprint arXiv:2409.01234*, 2024.

[112] V. R. Kumar, C. Eising, C. Witt, and S. K. Yogamani, "Surround-view fisheye camera perception for automated driving: Overview, survey & challenges," *IEEE Transactions on Intelligent Transportation Systems*, vol. 24, no. 4, pp. 3638–3659, 2023.

[113] A. D. M. Ibrahum, M. Hussain, and J.-E. Hong, "Deep learning adversarial attacks and defenses in autonomous vehicles: A systematic literature review from a safety perspective," *Artificial Intelligence Review*, vol. 58, no. 1, p. 28, 2024.

[114] D. Fernández Llorca, R. Hamon, H. Junklewitz, K. Grosse, L. Kunze, P. Seiniger, R. Swaim, N. Reed, A. Alahi, E. Gómez, *et al.*, "Testing autonomous vehicles and ai: perspectives and challenges from cybersecurity, transparency, robustness and fairness," *European Transport Research Review*, vol. 17, no. 1, p. 38, 2025.

[115] T. Sato, R. Suzuki, Y. Hayakawa, K. Ikeda, O. Sako, R. Nagata, R. Yoshida, Q. A. Chen, and K. Yoshioka, "On the realism of lidar spoofing attacks against autonomous driving vehicle at high speed and long distance," in *Proceedings of the Network and Distributed System Security Symposium (NDSS)*, 2025.

[116] T. Sato, Y. Hayakawa, R. Suzuki, Y. Shiiki, K. Yoshioka, and Q. A. Chen, "Lidar spoofing meets the new-gen: Capability improvements, broken assumptions, and new attack strategies," *arXiv preprint arXiv:2303.10555*, 2023.

[117] Y. Cao, S. H. Bhupathiraju, P. Naghavi, T. Sugawara, Z. M. Mao, and S. Rampazzi, "You can't see me: Physical removal attacks on {lidar-based} autonomous vehicles driving frameworks," in *32nd USENIX security symposium (USENIX Security 23)*, pp. 2993–3010, 2023.

[118] Y. Zhu, C. Miao, H. Xue, Y. Yu, L. Su, and C. Qiao, "Malicious attacks against multi-sensor fusion in autonomous driving," in *Proceedings of the 30th Annual International Conference on Mobile Computing and Networking*, pp. 436–451, 2024.

[119] E. Yeh, J. Choi, N. Prelcic, C. Bhat, and R. W. Heath Jr, "Security in automotive radar and vehicular networks," *submitted to Microwave Journal*, 2016.

[120] T. Fei, A. Becker, and M. Gardill, "Interference mitigation in automotive radar systems: A current state survey and future trends," *Authorea Preprints*.

[121] C. Aydogdu, M. F. Keskin, G. K. Carvajal, O. Eriksson, H. Hellsten, H. Herbertsson, E. Nilsson, M. Rydstrom, K. Vanas, and H. Wymeersch, "Radar interference mitigation for automated driving: Exploring proactive strategies," *IEEE Signal Processing Magazine*, vol. 37, no. 4, pp. 72–84, 2020.

[122] S. Dasgupta, A. Ahmed, M. Rahman, and T. N. Bandi, "Unveiling the stealthy threat: Analyzing slow drift gps spoofing attacks for autonomous vehicles in urban environments and enabling the resilience," *arXiv preprint arXiv:2401.01394*, 2024.

[123] J. Shen, J. Y. Won, Z. Chen, and Q. A. Chen, "Drift with devil: Security of {Multi-Sensor} fusion based localization in {High-Level} autonomous driving under {GPS} spoofing," in *29th USENIX security symposium (USENIX Security 20)*, pp. 931–948, 2020.

[124] J. M. Kang, T. S. Yoon, E. Kim, and J. B. Park, "Lane-level map-matching method for vehicle localization using gps and camera on a high-definition map," *Sensors*, vol. 20, no. 8, p. 2166, 2020.

[125] R. Sadli, M. Afkir, A. Hadid, A. Rivenq, and A. Taleb-Ahmed, "Map-matching-based localization using camera and low-cost gps for lane-level accuracy," *Sensors*, vol. 22, no. 7, p. 2434, 2022.

[126] A. Krayani, G. Barabino, L. Marcenaro, and C. Regazzoni, "Integrated sensing and communication for joint gps spoofing and jamming detection in vehicular v2x networks," in *2023 IEEE Wireless Communications and Networking Conference (WCNC)*, pp. 1–7, IEEE, 2023.

[127] M. Dai, H. Li, J. Liang, C. Zhang, X. Pan, Y. Tian, J. Cao, and Y. Wang, "Lane level positioning method for unmanned driving based on inertial system and vector map information fusion applicable to gnss denied environments," *Drones*, vol. 7, no. 4, p. 239, 2023.

[128] M. Amoozadeh, A. Raghuramu, C.-N. Chuah, D. Ghosal, H. M. Zhang, J. Rowe, and K. Levitt, "Security vulnerabilities of connected vehicle streams and their impact on cooperative driving," *IEEE Communications Magazine*, vol. 53, no. 6, pp. 126–132, 2015.

[129] X. Hu, T. Park, and K. G. Shin, "Attack-tolerant time-synchronization in wireless sensor networks," in *IEEE INFOCOM 2008-The 27th Conference on Computer Communications*, pp. 41–45, IEEE, 2008.

[130] S. Hussain, O. Chowdhury, S. Mehnaz, and E. Bertino, "Lteinspector: A systematic approach for adversarial testing of 4g lte," in *Network and Distributed Systems Security (NDSS) Symposium 2018*, 2018.

[131] C. Lai, R. Lu, D. Zheng, and X. Shen, "Security and privacy challenges in 5g-enabled vehicular networks," *IEEE Network*, vol. 34, no. 2, pp. 37–45, 2020.

[132] M. Chowdhury, M. Islam, and Z. Khan, "Security of connected and automated vehicles," *arXiv preprint arXiv:2012.13464*, 2020.

[133] A. Taeihagh and H. S. M. Lim, "Governing autonomous vehicles: emerging responses for safety, liability, privacy, cybersecurity, and industry risks," *Transport reviews*, vol. 39, no. 1, pp. 103–128, 2019.

[134] G. De La Torre, P. Rad, and K.-K. R. Choo, "Driverless vehicle security: Challenges and future research opportunities," *Future Generation Computer Systems*, vol. 108, pp. 1092–1111, 2020.

[135] F. A. Butt, J. N. Chattha, J. Ahmad, M. U. Zia, M. Rizwan, and I. H. Naqvi, "On the integration of enabling wireless technologies and sensor fusion for next-generation connected and autonomous vehicles," *IEEE access*, vol. 10, pp. 14643–14668, 2022.

[136] B. Gul and F. Ertam, "In-vehicle communication cyber security: A comprehensive review of challenges and solutions," *Vehicular Communications*, vol. 50, p. 100846, 2024.

[137] R. S. Rathore, C. Hewage, O. Kaiwartya, and J. Lloret, "In-vehicle communication cyber security: challenges and solutions," *Sensors*, vol. 22, no. 17, p. 6679, 2022.

[138] M. AL-KADRI, "Can-mirgu: a comprehensive can bus attack dataset from moving vehicles for intrusion detection system evaluation.,"

[139] H. Zwickel, J. N. Kemal, C. Kieninger, Y. Kutuvantavida, M. Lauermann, J. Rittershofer, R. Pajkovic, D. Lindt, S. Randel, W. Freude, and C. Koos, "Electrically packaged silicon-organic hybrid modulator for communication and microwave photonic applications," in *2018 Conference on Lasers and Electro-Optics (CLEO)*, pp. 1–2, 2018.

[140] X. Zhang, J. Li, J. Zhou, S. Zhang, J. Wang, Y. Yuan, J. Liu, and J. Li, "Vehicle-to-everything communication in intelligent connected vehicles: A survey and taxonomy," *Automotive Innovation*, pp. 1–33, 2025.

[141] K. Shima, K. Senoo, K. Goto, K. Maruta, and C.-J. Ahn, "Data-aided smi algorithm using common correlation matrix for adaptive array interference suppression," in *2019 25th Asia-Pacific Conference on Communications (APCC)*, pp. 398–402, 2019.

[142] M. R. Ansari, J. Petit, J.-P. Monteuuis, and C. Chen, "Vasp: V2x application spoofing platform," in *Proceedings Inaugural International Symposium on Vehicle Security & Privacy, ndss-symposium*, 2023.

[143] Z. Feng, T. Sun, and X. Tian, "Research on scara robot sorting system based on codesys," in *2019 Chinese Control And Decision Conference (CCDC)*, pp. 5611–5615, 2019.

[144] D. R. Junaidi, M. Ma, and R. Su, "Secure vehicular platoon management against sybil attacks," *Sensors*, vol. 22, no. 22, p. 9000, 2022.

[145] K. Grover, A. Lim, and Q. Yang, "Jamming and anti–jamming techniques in wireless networks: a survey," *International Journal of Ad Hoc and Ubiquitous Computing*, vol. 17, no. 4, pp. 197–215, 2014.

[146] T. Yoshizawa, D. Singelée, J. T. Muehlberg, S. Delbruel, A. Taherkordi, D. Hughes, and B. Preneel, "A survey of security and privacy issues in v2x communication systems," *ACM Computing Surveys*, vol. 55, no. 9, pp. 1–36, 2023.

[147] S. Dasgupta, M. Rahman, M. Islam, and M. Chowdhury, "A sensor fusion-based gnss spoofing attack detection framework for autonomous vehicles," *IEEE Transactions on Intelligent Transportation Systems*, vol. 23, no. 12, pp. 23559–23572, 2022.

[148] N. Trkulja, D. Starobinski, and R. A. Berry, "Denial-of-service attacks on c-v2x networks," *arXiv preprint arXiv:2010.13725*, 2020.

[149] Z. H. Khattak, B. L. Smith, and M. D. Fontaine, "Impact of cyberattacks on safety and stability of connected and automated vehicle platoons under lane changes," *Accident Analysis & Prevention*, vol. 150, p. 105861, 2021.

[150] M. Sadaf, Z. Iqbal, A. R. Javed, I. Saba, M. Krichen, S. Majeed, and A. Raza, "Connected and automated vehicles: Infrastructure, applications, security, critical challenges, and future aspects," *Technologies*, vol. 11, no. 5, p. 117, 2023.

[151] J. Canelas, "Adequate performance for real-time processing in autonomous vehicles," 07 2025.

[152] D. J. Yeong, G. Velasco-Hernandez, J. Barry, and J. Walsh, "Sensor and sensor fusion technology in autonomous vehicles: A review," 02 2021.

[153] M. Hasanujjaman, M. Z. Chowdhury, and Y. M. Jang, "Sensor fusion in autonomous vehicle with traffic surveillance camera system: detection, localization, and ai networking," *Sensors*, vol. 23, no. 6, p. 3335, 2023.

[154] NVIDIA, "Accelerating the pony av sensor data processing pipeline." `https://developer.nvidia.com/blog/accelerating-the-pony-av-sensor-data-processing-pipeline/?utm_source=chatgpt.com`, 2022. Accessed: Sep, 2025].

[155] M. Muhammad, P. Kearney, A. Aneiba, and A. Kunz, "Analysis of security overhead in broadcast v2v communications," in *International conference on computer safety, reliability, and security*, pp. 251–263, Springer, 2019.

[156] H. Zhang, S. Li, Z. Li, M. Anis, D. Lord, and Y. Zhou, "Why anticipatory sensing matters in commercial acc systems under cut-in scenarios: A perspective from stochastic safety analysis," *Accident Analysis & Prevention*, vol. 218, p. 108064, 2025.

[157] Q. Xia, L. Chen, X. Xu, Y. Cai, H. Jiang, and G. Pan, "Expected yaw rate–based trajectory tracking control with vision delay for intelligent vehicle," *Science Progress*, vol. 103, no. 3, p. 0036850420934274, 2020.

[158] C. Wang, R. Song, R. Muller, J.-P. Monteuuis, Z. B. Celik, J. Petit, R. Gerdes, and M. Li, "Cp-freezer: Latency attacks against vehicular cooperative perception," *arXiv preprint arXiv:2508.01062*, 2025.

[159] L. Lin, H. Ge, and R. Cheng, "Heterogeneous traffic flow model under connected vehicles environment considering cyberattacks," *Modern Physics Letters B*, vol. 36, no. 01, p. 2150537, 2022.

[160] Y. Li, Y. Tu, Q. Fan, C. Dong, and W. Wang, "Influence of cyber-attacks on longitudinal safety of connected and automated vehicles," *Accident Analysis & Prevention*, vol. 121, pp. 148–156, 2018.

[161] Z. Sun, R. Liu, H. Hu, D. Liu, and Z. Yan, "Cyberattacks on connected automated vehicles: a traffic impact analysis. iet intell transp syst 17 (2): 295–311," 2023.

[162] Radware, "Application layer (osi layer 7) ddos attack?," 2023. Accessed: 2025-08-27.

[163] CCI-CVN, "Self-driving cars: Cruising towards a secure future," 2023. Accessed: 2025-08-27.

[164] Z. El-Rewini, K. Sadatsharan, D. F. Selvaraj, S. J. Plathottam, and P. Ranganathan, "Cybersecurity challenges in vehicular communications," *Vehicular Communications*, vol. 23, p. 100214, 2020.

[165] S. Ur Rehman, M. Khaliq, S. I. Imtiaz, A. Rasool, M. Shafiq, A. R. Javed, Z. Jalil, and A. K. Bashir, "Diddos: An approach for detection and identification of distributed denial of service (ddos) cyberattacks using gated recurrent units (gru)," *Future Generation Computer Systems*, vol. 118, pp. 453–466, 2021.

[166] P. Moriano, S. C. Hespeler, M. Li, and M. Mahbub, "Adaptive anomaly detection for identifying attacks in cyber-physical systems: A systematic literature review," *Artificial Intelligence Review*, vol. 58, no. 9, p. 283, 2025.

[167] T. Ni, X. Gu, H. Wang, and Y. Li, "Real-time detection of application-layer ddos attack using time series analysis," *Journal of Control Science and Engineering*, vol. 2013, no. 1, p. 821315, 2013.

[168] L. Kleinrock, *Queueing Systems, Volume I: Theory*. New York: Wiley-Interscience, 1975.

[169] J. F. Shortle, J. M. Thompson, D. Gross, and C. M. Harris, *Fundamentals of Queueing Theory*. Wiley Series in Probability and Statistics, Hoboken, NJ: John Wiley & Sons, 5 ed., 2018.

[170] M. Harchol-Balter, *Performance Modeling and Design of Computer Systems: Queueing Theory in Action*. Cambridge: Cambridge University Press, 2013.

Appendices

A Analytical Proof of the Velocity–Density Relationship Shape

This section provides an analytical justification for the shape of the velocity–density diagram shown in Figure 2(a). The queueing-based velocity function consists of three distinct regimes: a constant region at low densities, a discrete drop at the transition point $k = 1/r$, and a continuously decreasing branch that is concave upward for $k > 1/r$.

For $k \leq 1/r$, differentiating with respect to k gives: $\frac{\partial V}{\partial k} = 0$, Thus, V remains constant across the low-density region, corresponding to the horizontal branch in the diagram.

At $k = 1/r$, vehicles begin to enter the cooperative regime where the detection delay becomes active. Since the denominator for $V(1/r^{+})$ gets larger, producing a discrete drop in velocity.

Beyond the transition, both detection and decision queues contribute to the total delay. Let the denominator of the velocity in this regime in Equation 9 be denoted by kD, where $D > 0$. Differentiating with respect to k:

$$\frac{\partial V}{\partial k} = \frac{-\ell kD - (1 - k\ell)\frac{\partial(kD)}{\partial k}}{(kD)^2}. \tag{38}$$

Only the decision-stage delay term within D depends on k:

$$\frac{1}{\mu_t - \left(\frac{kr-1}{k(r-\ell)}(1-\alpha)\lambda_v + \lambda_t\right)}. \tag{39}$$

The derivative of its inner fraction is:

$$\frac{\partial}{\partial k}\left(\frac{kr-1}{k(r-\ell)}\right) = \frac{1}{k^2(r-\ell)} > 0, \tag{40}$$

indicating that the delay term increases with k. Substituting into Eq. (38) yields: $\frac{\partial V}{\partial k} < 0$. Velocity therefore decreases monotonically with density in the cooperative regime.

Differentiating once more gives:

$$\frac{\partial^2 V}{\partial k^2} = \frac{-2\frac{\partial(kD)}{\partial k}\left(\ell kD + (1-k\ell)\frac{\partial(kD)}{\partial k}\right) - (1-k\ell)kD\frac{\partial^2(kD)}{\partial k^2}}{(kD)^3}. \tag{41}$$

Because the second derivative of the delay term is positive:

$$\frac{\partial^2}{\partial k^2}\left(\frac{1}{\mu_t - \lambda_t - \frac{kr-1}{k(r-\ell)}(1-\alpha)\lambda_v}\right) > 0, \tag{42}$$

it follows that $\frac{\partial^2 V}{\partial k^2} > 0$. Hence, the velocity curve is concave upward in this region, approaching zero asymptotically.

B Analytical Proof of the Flow–Density Relationship Shape

This section provides an analytical justification for the shape of the flow–density diagram presented in Figure 2(b). The queueing-based flow function exhibits three distinct behaviors across density regimes: a linear increase at low densities, a discontinuous drop at the transition point $k = 1/r$, and a nonlinear concave downward decrease beyond that point.

In regime $k \leq 1/r$, differentiating with respect to k gives:

$$\frac{\partial Q}{\partial k} = \frac{r-\ell}{\frac{1}{\mu_t-\lambda_t}+T} > 0, \qquad \frac{\partial^2 Q}{\partial k^2} = 0. \tag{43}$$

Hence, Q increases linearly with density, forming the ascending branch in the diagram.

At $k = 1/r$, the system transitions from the non-cooperative to the cooperative regime. The detection-stage queuing delay activates, increasing the denominator of the velocity expression. Evaluating flow on both sides of the transition. Since the denominator for $Q(1/r^+)$ gets larger due to the additional queueing term, producing the discrete drop observed in the diagram.

Beyond the transition, both detection and decision delays depend on density, and the flow becomes nonlinear. Let the denominator of Equation 10 in this regime, be D. Differentiating gives:

$$\frac{\partial Q}{\partial k} = \frac{-\ell D - (1-k\ell)\frac{\partial D}{\partial k}}{D^2}. \tag{44a}$$

The only k-dependent term inside D is:

$$\frac{1}{\mu_t - \left(\frac{kr-1}{k(r-\ell)}(1-\alpha)\lambda_v + \lambda_t\right)}, \tag{44b}$$

whose derivative is:

$$\frac{\partial}{\partial k}\left(\frac{1}{\mu_t - \left(\frac{kr-1}{k(r-\ell)}(1-\alpha)\lambda_v + \lambda_t\right)}\right) = \frac{(1-\alpha)\lambda_v}{(r-\ell)k^2\left[\mu_t - \lambda_t - \frac{kr-1}{k(r-\ell)}(1-\alpha)\lambda_v\right]^2} > 0. \tag{44c}$$

Hence $\frac{\partial D}{\partial k} > 0$ and $D > 0$, leading to $\frac{\partial Q}{\partial k} < 0$. The flow therefore decreases monotonically as density increases.

Differentiating again yields:

$$\frac{\partial^2 Q}{\partial k^2} = \frac{-2\frac{\partial D}{\partial k}(\ell D + (1-k\ell)\frac{\partial D}{\partial k}) - (1-k\ell)D\frac{\partial^2 D}{\partial k^2}}{D^3}. \tag{45}$$

The second derivative of the delay term is:

$$\frac{\partial^2}{\partial k^2}\left(\frac{1}{\mu_t - \lambda_t - \frac{kr-1}{k(r-\ell)}(1-\alpha)\lambda_v}\right) = \frac{2(\lambda')^2 + (\mu_t - \lambda_t - \lambda)\lambda''}{(\mu_t - \lambda_t - \lambda)^3}, \tag{46a}$$

where

$$\lambda' = \frac{(1-\alpha)\lambda_v}{k^2(r-\ell)} > 0, \quad \lambda'' = -\frac{2(1-\alpha)\lambda_v}{k^3(r-\ell)} < 0. \tag{46b}$$

The positive term $2(\lambda')^2$ dominates, implying $\frac{\partial^2 D}{\partial k^2} > 0$, and therefore $\frac{\partial^2 Q}{\partial k^2} < 0$. So, the flow is concave downward in this regime.

C Concavity Proof of the FCC Objective Function

This section provides a proof that the objective function of the FCC optimization problem is concave. Concavity is established if the Hessian of the objective function is negative semi-definite, meaning all eigenvalues are non-positive.

The objective function is:

$$f(\mu_v,\mu_t) = \frac{1}{S} \cdot \frac{\min(S,r)-\ell}{\tau}, \tag{47}$$

where the total delay τ is given by Equation (26), and we also refer to the previously defined arrival rate at the decision-making station as λ_{eff}:

$$\lambda_t^{\text{eff}} = \beta(S)(1-\alpha)\lambda_v(S)+\lambda_t. \tag{48}$$

Case I. $S < r$

In this case, the total delay at the detection and decision-making stations is expressed as

$$g(\mu_v,\mu_t) = \frac{1}{\mu_v-\lambda_v^{\text{det}}} + \frac{1}{\mu_t-\lambda_t^{\text{eff}}} + T, \tag{49}$$

and the corresponding objective function becomes

$$f(\mu_v,\mu_t) = \frac{S-\ell}{S} \cdot \frac{1}{g(\mu_v,\mu_t)}. \tag{50a}$$

So that

$$\frac{\partial g}{\partial \mu_v} = -\frac{1}{(\mu_v-\lambda_v^{\text{det}})^2}, \quad \frac{\partial g}{\partial \mu_t} = -\frac{1}{(\mu_t-\lambda_t^{\text{eff}})^2}, \tag{50b}$$

$$\frac{\partial f}{\partial \mu_v} = -\frac{\frac{S-\ell}{S}\cdot\frac{\partial g}{\partial \mu_v}}{g^2} = -\frac{\frac{S-\ell}{S}\cdot\frac{1}{(\mu_v-\lambda_v^{\text{det}})^2}}{g^2}, \tag{50c}$$

$$\frac{\partial f}{\partial \mu_t} = -\frac{\frac{S-\ell}{S}\cdot\frac{\partial g}{\partial \mu_t}}{g^2} = -\frac{\frac{S-\ell}{S}\cdot\frac{1}{(\mu_t-\lambda_t^{\text{eff}})^2}}{g^2}, \tag{50d}$$

$$\frac{\partial^2 f}{\partial \mu_v^2} = \frac{\frac{S-\ell}{S}\left[-\frac{2g^2}{(\mu_v-\lambda_v^{\text{det}})^3} + \frac{2g}{(\mu_v-\lambda_v^{\text{det}})^4}\right]}{g^4}, \tag{50e}$$

$$\frac{\partial^2 f}{\partial \mu_t^2} = \frac{\frac{S-\ell}{S}\left[-\frac{2g^2}{(\mu_t-\lambda_t^{\text{eff}})^3} + \frac{2g}{(\mu_t-\lambda_t^{\text{eff}})^4}\right]}{g^4}, \tag{50f}$$

$$\frac{\partial^2 f}{\partial \mu_v \partial \mu_t} = 0, \tag{50g}$$

Thus, the Hessian is diagonal:

$$H = \begin{bmatrix} \frac{\partial^2 f}{\partial \mu_v^2} & 0 \\ 0 & \frac{\partial^2 f}{\partial \mu_t^2} \end{bmatrix} \tag{51}$$

The dominant term in both diagonal elements is negative, and since $\frac{S-\ell}{S} > 0$ and $g^4 > 0$, both eigenvalues are negative. Therefore, the Hessian is negative semi-definite, confirming concavity.

Case II. S$\geq r$

In this case, the corresponding objective function becomes:

$$f(\mu_v, \mu_t) = \frac{r-\ell}{S} \cdot \frac{1}{\frac{1}{\mu_t-\lambda_t} + T}, \tag{52a}$$

$$\frac{\partial f}{\partial \mu_v} = 0, \quad \frac{\partial f}{\partial \mu_t} = -\frac{\frac{r-\ell}{S}}{(\mu_t - \lambda_t)^2 \left(\frac{1}{\mu_t-\lambda_t} + T\right)^2}, \tag{52b}$$

$$\frac{\partial^2 f}{\partial \mu_v^2} = 0, \quad \frac{\partial^2 f}{\partial \mu_t^2} = \frac{\frac{r-\ell}{S} \cdot \left[-\frac{2\left(\frac{1}{\mu_t-\lambda_t}+T\right)^2}{(\mu_t-\lambda_t)^3} + \text{other terms}\right]}{\left(\frac{1}{\mu_t-\lambda_t} + T\right)^4} < 0, \tag{52c}$$

$$\frac{\partial^2 f}{\partial \mu_v \partial \mu_t} = 0, \tag{52d}$$

The eigenvalues are 0 and the negative μ_t term, so the Hessian is negative semi-definite.

For both $S < r$ and $S \geq r$, all eigenvalues of the Hessian are non-positive. Hence, the objective function is concave over the feasible region defined by $\mu_v + \mu_t = C$ and other constraints. This guarantees the existence of a global maximum for the FCC model under adversarial load with malicious packet processing.

D Proof of Lemma 1

Since the numerator $\min(S,r)-\ell$ is constant at fixed S, maximizing $\big(\min(S,r)-\ell\big)/\tau$ is equivalent to minimizing the delay τ. Define

$$a := \lambda_v^{\text{det}} = \lambda_v\big[(1-\alpha)+C_m\alpha\big], \tag{53a}$$

$$b := \lambda_t + \beta(S)\big(1-\alpha)\lambda_v(S), \tag{53b}$$

with $\beta(S)$ and $\lambda_v(S)$ defined in Equations (5) and (1), respectively.

The capacity constraint is $\mu_v+\mu_t = C$, and stability requires $\mu_v > a$ and $\mu_t > b$ whenever the corresponding stage is active.

Case I. $S < r$

We introduce the positive slacks $x := \mu_v - a$ and $y := \mu_t - b$, so that

$$\tau = T + \frac{1}{x} + \frac{1}{y}, \tag{54a}$$

$$x + y = H, \tag{54b}$$

$$H := C - (a+b). \tag{54c}$$

The minimization $\min\{\,1/x + 1/y :\ x > 0,\ y > 0,\ x+y = H\,\}$ is convex and symmetric. The KKT conditions enforce equal slacks at the optimum, $x^* = y^* = H/2$ (feasible if $H > 0$). Substituting back gives the closed forms

$$\mu_v^* = \frac{C+a-b}{2}, \tag{55a}$$

$$\mu_t^* = \frac{C-a+b}{2}. \tag{55b}$$

valid exactly when $H = C-(a+b) > 0$; otherwise at least one slack is non-positive and τ diverges. Writing a and b explicitly gives the $S < r$ branch of the Equations (23) and (24).

Case II. $S \geq r$

In this case. the detection stage is inactive ($\beta(S) = 0$, $\lambda_v(S) = 0$); we enforce $\mu_v^* = 0$ and the capacity constraint gives $\mu_t^* = C$. Stability then requires $C > \lambda_t$, and the delay reduces to

$$\mu_v^* = 0, \tag{56a}$$

$$\mu_t^* = C. \tag{56b}$$

These expressions make the dependence on α transparent through $a(\alpha)$ and $b(S, \alpha)$: increasing α expands the detection load a via C_m and, depending on ε and $\beta(S)$, can increase or decrease the decision-stage effective load b. The feasibility margins $C > (a+b)$ for $S < r$ and $C > \lambda_t$ for $S \geq r$ are the exact thresholds for finite delay.

E Concavity Proof of the CAC Objective Function

This appendix provides a proof that the objective function of the CAC optimization problem is concave. The objective function is:

$$f(\mu_v, \mu_t) = \frac{1}{S} \cdot \frac{\min(S, r) - \ell}{\tau} - C_1\mu_v - C_2\mu_t \tag{57}$$

where the total delay τ and the effective arrival rate at the decision-making station are given by Equations (26) and (48), respectively.

Case I. $S < r$

By substituting Equation (49), the objective function can be rewritten as:

$$f(\mu_v, \mu_t) = \frac{\frac{S-\ell}{S}}{g(\mu_v, \mu_t)} - C_1\mu_v - C_2\mu_t. \tag{58}$$

The first-order derivatives of the first term are:

$$\frac{\partial}{\partial \mu_v}\left(\frac{S-\ell}{Sg}\right) = -\frac{\frac{S-\ell}{S}}{g^2} \cdot \frac{1}{(\mu_v - \lambda_v^{\text{det}})^2}, \tag{59a}$$

$$\frac{\partial}{\partial \mu_t}\left(\frac{S-\ell}{Sg}\right) = -\frac{\frac{S-\ell}{S}}{g^2} \cdot \frac{1}{(\mu_t - \lambda_t^{\text{eff}})^2}. \tag{59b}$$

The second-order derivatives are:

$$\frac{\partial^2 f}{\partial \mu_v^2} = \frac{\frac{S-\ell}{S}\left[-2g^2/(\mu_v - \lambda_v^{\text{det}})^3 + 2g/(\mu_v - \lambda_v^{\text{det}})^4\right]}{g^4} < 0 \tag{60a}$$

$$\frac{\partial^2 f}{\partial \mu_t^2} = \frac{\frac{S-\ell}{S}\left[-2g^2/(\mu_t - \lambda_t^{\text{eff}})^3 + 2g/(\mu_t - \lambda_t^{\text{eff}})^4\right]}{g^4} < 0 \tag{60b}$$

$$\frac{\partial^2 f}{\partial \mu_v \partial \mu_t} = 0 \tag{60c}$$

Thus the Hessian is diagonal with negative entries, confirming negative semi-definiteness. Therefore, $f(\mu_v, \mu_t)$ is concave when $S < r$.

Case II. $S \geq r$

In this regime, $\mu_v = 0$ and $\lambda_v(S) = 0$, so the objective reduces to:

$$f(\mu_t) = \frac{\frac{r-\ell}{S}}{\frac{1}{\mu_t - \lambda_t} + T} - C_2 \mu_t. \tag{61}$$

The first derivative is:

$$\frac{df}{d\mu_t} = -\frac{\frac{r-\ell}{S} \cdot \frac{1}{(\mu_t - \lambda_t)^2}}{\left(\frac{1}{\mu_t - \lambda_t} + T\right)^2} - C_2, \tag{62a}$$

and the second derivative is:

$$\frac{d^2 f}{d\mu_t^2} = -\frac{\frac{r-\ell}{S} \cdot \left[2/(\mu_t - \lambda_t)^3 \left(\frac{1}{\mu_t - \lambda_t} + T\right)^2 + 2/(\mu_t - \lambda_t)^4 \left(\frac{1}{\mu_t - \lambda_t} + T\right)\right]}{\left(\frac{1}{\mu_t - \lambda_t} + T\right)^4} < 0. \tag{62b}$$

Hence, the objective is concave in the feasible interval for μ_t when $S \geq r$.

Since the objective function is concave for both $S < r$ and $S \geq r$, and the feasible set is convex, the CAC optimization problem admits a unique global maximum.

F Proof of Lemma 2

In this section, we present the solution to the optimization problem defined in Equation (25), where the total delay τ is given by Equation (26), subject to the box constraints $0 \le \mu_v \le \mu_v^{\max}$ and $0 \le \mu_t \le \mu_t^{\max}$.

Case I. $S < r$

The slack variables are:

$$x := \mu_v - \lambda_v\left[(1-\alpha) + C_m\alpha\right] > 0, \tag{63a}$$

$$y := \mu_t - \left\{\lambda_t + \left(1 - \tfrac{S-\ell}{r-\ell}\right)(1-\alpha)\lambda_v\right\} > 0. \tag{63b}$$

so $\tau = T + \frac{1}{x} + \frac{1}{y}$, while the geometric factor in the objective is $(S-\ell)/S$. The first-order optimality conditions (with inactive caps) give:

$$\frac{(S-\ell)/S}{\tau^2 x^2} = C_1, \tag{64a}$$

$$\frac{(S-\ell)/S}{\tau^2 y^2} = C_2, \tag{64b}$$

$$x = \frac{\sqrt{(S-\ell)/(SC_1)}}{\tau}, \tag{64c}$$

$$y = \frac{\sqrt{(S-\ell)/(SC_2)}}{\tau}. \tag{64d}$$

Substituting into $\tau = T + \frac{1}{x} + \frac{1}{y}$ yields:

$$\tau = \frac{T}{1-\rho(S)}, \tag{65a}$$

$$\rho(S) = \sqrt{\frac{C_1 S}{S-\ell}} + \sqrt{\frac{C_2 S}{S-\ell}}, \tag{65b}$$

and the interior increments:

$$\Delta_v(S) = \frac{1}{T}\sqrt{\frac{S-\ell}{SC_1}}(1-\rho(S)), \tag{66a}$$

$$\Delta_t(S) = \frac{1}{T}\sqrt{\frac{S-\ell}{SC_2}}(1-\rho(S)). \tag{66b}$$

Let the cap rooms be $U_v = \mu_v^{\max} - \lambda_v[(1-\alpha)+C_m\alpha]$ and $U_t = \mu_t^{\max} - \{\lambda_t + [1-\frac{S-\ell}{r-\ell}](1-\alpha)\lambda_v\}$. When $0 < \rho(S) < 1$ and $\Delta_v(S) \le U_v$, $\Delta_t(S) \le U_t$, the interior solution is:

$$\mu_v^* = \lambda_v[(1-\alpha)+C_m\alpha] + \Delta_v(S), \tag{67a}$$

$$\mu_t^* = \lambda_t + \left(1-\tfrac{S-\ell}{r-\ell}\right)(1-\alpha)\lambda_v + \Delta_t(S). \tag{67b}$$

If the interior point violates a single cap, complementary slackness activates that cap and the remaining variable solves a one-dimensional stationarity. When the detection cap binds ($\mu_v^* = \mu_v^{\max}$), write $C_m = T + 1/U_v$ and obtain:

$$\mu_t^* = \lambda_t + \left(1-\tfrac{S-\ell}{r-\ell}\right)(1-\alpha)\lambda_v + \min\left\{\max\left(\frac{\sqrt{\frac{S-\ell}{SC_2}}-1}{C_m}, 0\right), U_t\right\}. \tag{68}$$

When the decision cap binds ($\mu_t^* = \mu_t^{\max}$), write $K_t = T + 1/U_t$ and obtain

$$\mu_v^* = \lambda_v[(1-\alpha)+C_m\alpha] + \min\left\{\max\left(\frac{\sqrt{\frac{S-\ell}{SC_1}}-1}{K_t}, 0\right), U_v\right\}. \tag{69}$$

If $\Delta_v(S) > U_v$ and $\Delta_t(S) > U_t$, then complementary slackness gives

$$\mu_v^* = \mu_v^{\max}, \tag{70a}$$

$$\mu_t^* = \mu_t^{\max}. \tag{70b}$$

If $\rho(S) \ge 1$ or a clipped increment is non-positive, the penalties dominate and the optimum sits at the stability bounds:

$$\mu_v^* = \lambda_v[(1-\alpha) + C_m\alpha], \tag{71a}$$

$$\mu_t^* = \lambda_t + \left(1 - \tfrac{S-\ell}{r-\ell}\right)(1-\alpha)\lambda_v. \tag{71b}$$

Case II. $S \geq r$

we enforce $\mu_v^* = 0$ and the problem reduces to a single variable $x = \mu_t - \lambda_t > 0$ with benefit factor $(r-\ell)/S$. The stationary point solves $Tx + 1 = \sqrt{(r-\ell)/(SC_2)}$, i.e.

$$x_0 = \frac{\sqrt{\frac{r-\ell}{SC_2}} - 1}{T}, \tag{72}$$

which is then clipped to the feasible interval $[0,\ \mu_t^{\max} - \lambda_t]$, giving the final out-of-range solution

$$\mu_v^* = 0, \tag{73a}$$

$$\mu_t^* = \lambda_t + \min\left\{ \max\left(\frac{\sqrt{\frac{r-\ell}{SC_2}} - 1}{T}, 0 \right),\ \mu_t^{\max} - \lambda_t \right\}. \tag{73b}$$

These case-wise expressions are the KKT optima for the penalized, capped allocation with the enforced rule $\mu_v = 0$ when $S \geq r$.

G Nomenclature

C_1	Cost per unit of detection capacity
C_2	Cost per unit of decision-making capacity
C_m	Relative processing cost of a malicious V2V packet in detection station compared to a benign packe
C	Total computational capacity
ℓ	Safety margin distance
Q	Flow of vehicles
r	Range of the V2V communication
S	Spacing between a vehicle and its preceding vehicle
T	Fixed execution or processing time
W_v	processing delay in the detection station
W_t	processing delay in the decision-making station
λ_v	Arrival rate of V2V data packets at the detection station
λ_t	Arrival rate of V2I and sensor data at the decision-making station
λ_{total}	Arrival rate of refined V2V data, V2I and sensor data at the decision-making station
α	Ratio of malicious data in V2V data
β	Importance level of the refined V2V data
μ_v	Processing capacity of detection station
μ_t	Processing capacity of decision-making station
τ	Total processing delay in the system